Miami, Fort Lauderdale & Key West

Miami, Fort Lauderdale & Key West

By David G Taylor

Published by Thomas Cook Publishing
PO Box 227
The Thomas Cook Business Park
Coningsby Road
Peterborough
PE3 8XX

Email: books@thomascook.com

ISBN: 1841571 636

For Thomas Cook Publishing
Managing Director: Kevin Fitzgerald
Publisher: Donald Greig
Commissioning Editor: Deborah Parker
Editor: Sarah Hudson
Proofreader: Jan Wiltshire

For Pink Paper
General Manager: David Bridle
Publishing Manager: Mike Ross
Editor: Steve Anthony
Additional picture research: Claire Benjamin

Design: Studio 183 and Grassverge
Layout: Studio 183, Peterborough
Cover Design: Studio 183 and Grassverge
Cover Artwork: Steve Clarke, Studio 183

City maps drawn by: Steve Munns

Scanning: Dale Carrington, Chronos Publishing; David Bruce Graphics

Printed and bound in Spain by: Artes Gráficas Elkar, Loiu, Spain

Written and researched by David G. Taylor

Photography: Gavin Harrison

The following are thanked for supplying photographs, to whom the copyright belongs:
Dennis Dean.com: page 100 (Royal Palms)
Greater Fort Lauderdale Convention and Visitors Bureau: pages 65; 75 (flamingo); 76; 78; 89.
Florida Keys Tourism Development: pages 123; 125.
Neil Setchfield: page 107.

Cover photographs: Gavin Harrison, Scott Nunn.

Contents

CONTENTS

My Kind of Place...

Hi and welcome to *Out Around Miami, Fort Lauderdale and Key West*, a guide designed to help you get the most out of your stay by recommending the very best South Florida has to offer the lesbian and gay traveller. And what makes me qualified to judge, I hear you ask? Well, I'm a dedicated clubber, foodie and practising Friend of Dorothy. I've also just spent quite some time running around South Florida experiencing the high and especially the low life just for your benefit.

Credentials-wise, I'm the London Correspondent for Australia's cult queer visual arts magazine *(not only) blue* – for which I regularly write scurrilous lesbian and gay-flavoured travel features on countless destinations including Miami, Fort Lauderdale, London, Liverpool and Manchester, New York, Washington DC, Benidorm, Brussels, Ibiza and Las Vegas.

At home in the UK, I'm the Gay Correspondent for the *London Evening Standard* newspaper's weekly listings magazine *Hot Tickets*, reporting on the most exciting London-based gay and lesbian nightlife, events, theatre, film, literature, festivals and happenings. I've been an editor on *Fluid* magazine, where I organised and directed fashion editorials, and reported on anything from underground movies and club events to gay travel hotspots. As a writer/journalist, I've also written for *Attitude*, the *Evening Standard*, the *Independent*, *Boyz*, the *Pink Paper*, *Dazed & Confused* and *Time Out*.

This book isn't meant to be all-inclusive, but rather to save you time and money by pointing you in the direction of the accommodation, sights, shops and clubs which are most worth a look when you're in town. Sadly, as I discovered during my research, gay doesn't always mean quality, so while I've provided details of the better gay options in town, I've also included some of the better-quality, gay-friendly alternatives, plus a few surprises! While not all the places listed are gay owned and run, all are very gay-friendly. I hope you find it useful. Enjoy!

Art Deco Ocean Drive

Out in Miami, Fort Lauderdale & Key West

Gay-friendly South Florida affords lesbian and gay travellers a unique experience. While the sunshine blazes between the mid-20°F and low 30's all year round, all over the state, Miami, Fort Lauderdale and Key West provide three completely and utterly different holiday destinations within a relatively small portion of the United States. Each destination has its own relative merits, and I highly recommend that, on your first visit at least, you make the effort to sample a little of each.

The Miami gay scene, for instance, which centres on the southern tip of Miami Beach island, known as South Beach (or SoBe), is by far the most hip and happening, characterised by annual circuit parties, unbeatable alfresco dining and a wealth of firm, muscular boys and beautiful girls. South Beach is particularly cosmopolitan, and should be visited for its unique outdoor lifestyle, some truly excellent restaurants, a great white sandy gay beach and spectacularly pretty art-deco architecture. Just walking along the streets taking in the people and sights is an adventure in itself, and there's always plenty to see and do day

or night – whether you're up for a sophisticated drink at the brilliantly quirky Beauty Bar, or hanging out in Flamingo Park ogling the locals as they work up a daily sweat on the basketball courts.

Each place also has its drawbacks and I won't attempt to gloss over these either. Despite much to recommend it, personally I did find the club scene in SoBe to be a little predictable and regimented. If you like an unchallenging formula of muscle-boys and hands-in-the-air house and techno, then you're in for fun.

But with a few notable exceptions, most Miami bars and clubs seem to be carbon copies of their competitors, populated by the same aloof muscle crowd and music policies. Sure, there's a place for dance clubs, but there's also room for a little diversity, and unlike most cities, Miami's gay club-goers have yet to wake up to the joys of indie, pop, retro, underground garage, r'n'b, hip hop, funk, soul and tribal house.

In stark contrast, Key West has a much more sedate and casual pace, and takes itself much less seriously. It's really just a sleepy gay-friendly backwater. There's a

Party!

number of gay guest houses, but with only a handful of bars and clubs, there's not as much nightlife as you might have expected, given the town's reputation as a premier gay hotspot. Get over the idea that you can cover the whole gay scene in one evening, and just enjoy the relaxation of life in the slow lane.

It has to be said that those bars and clubs that do exist are lively and relatively diverse: including a leather bar, a popular Sunday tea dance, two drag bars, a male revue and a packed video bar.

The gay nightlife is all well within bar-hopping distance, which'll keep your evenings from turning stale. Had enough of one venue? Then just move on to the next. Beautiful Key West really is the place to escape from the pressures of life, and is particularly popular with the 30–40-plus crowd, especially holidaying same-sex couples.

If it's fast living you're after, Fort Lauderdale, on the other hand, is America's newest must-see and best-kept secret, rapidly taking over as Florida's queer capital with the biggest and best gay scene in the state.

Unusually, thriving leather, bar and dance scenes exist happily

side by side, making the nightlife extremely varied – which I guess reflects the city's particularly diverse, and generally slightly older 32-plus gay population.

One drawback though; unlike Key West and Miami Beach, Fort Lauderdale is designed for the motor car. Of course this means that almost everything is unbelievably spread out, and as the public transportation system (a few unfathomably infrequent buses) leaves a lot to be desired, you absolutely need to hire a car for the duration of your stay, or else be prepared to fork out on multiple taxi rides every day.

Once you have your wheels, however, the city completely opens up into a different experience, presenting you with loads of queer options. There's a choice of four gay beaches, scores of gay and gay-friendly stores, some great dance clubs and video bars, a very cruisey leather scene and dozens of gay resorts and guest houses.

South Beach clubbers, tired of

Boats and palm trees

the dance music and those same old faces, often load up the car with friends and make the 30- to 40-minute pilgrimage to Fort Lauderdale for those very reasons.

South Beach – flying the rainbow flag

South Beach, Miami Beach & Mainland Miami

Miami Beach is an island just off the coast of mainland Miami connected via a series of bridges or causeways. Miami's gay scene is located almost entirely on the southernmost tip of Miami Beach, known as South Beach, or SoBe to the locals. Although there are a few clubs and sights to explore on the mainland, everything you could possibly need for your stay is within walking distance on South Beach. Most SoBe residents rarely cross to the mainland, and you probably won't need to bother either.

It's not hard to see why. South Beach is extremely pretty. Lushly vegetated, its palms, figs, vines, hibiscus, bougainvillea and jasmine compete for space with over 800 art-deco properties in modern ice-cream pastel shades. Tiny gecko lizards dart away whenever you tread too close, while dragonflies and bright yellow Yeliconia butterflies buzz by.

It's this chocolate-box beauty that has made SoBe and mainland Miami a favourite backdrop for film and TV shows. The cult 1980s TV cop show *Miami Vice* was based here and James Bond battled his arch-enemy Goldfinger in style at the exclusive Fontainebleau Hotel.

Home to the beautiful and moneyed, New York's elite come here to see and be seen. A lethal combination of the sun-worshipping, body-conscious beach culture and muscular circuit-party queens means that the population is obsessed with looks. Look at the human traffic around you, and – if you're not rich, beautiful, buff and bronzed yourself – you may even catch yourself feeling a little insecure.

Skating along South Beach

Stepping Out

While there are things over on the mainland worth a visit, by far the coolest, most exciting, and most queer-friendly part of Miami is SoBe (South Beach). With it's pretty, pastel-coloured Art Deco buildings, wide sandy beaches, pavement restuarants and quirky shops there plenty to see and do here alone. Depending on the pace of your holiday and the length of your stay you might be content to restrict your explorations to SoBe. Read on for a cross-section of the best SoBe has to offer, and a smattering of distractions from mainland Miami. If you fancy venturing further afield you can find more sights and sounds on the Greater Miami Convention & Visitors Bureau website at www.tropicoolmiami.com, or call for a copy of their Vacation Planner on 305 539 3000.

My Top Sights

Art Deco District

Art Deco detail

🛈 Art Deco Welcome Center, 1001 Ocean Drive, Miami Beach
📞 305-672-2014

The Art Deco District offers the largest collection of art-deco architecture in the world within one square mile. Built in the 1930s and 40s, there are about 800 art-deco homes, hotels and structures still remaining. Most of them were repainted in non-authentic ice-cream pastels during the 1980s.

A selection of the most interesting buildings is taken in during the 90-minute walking tour which sets off from the Art Deco Welcome Center on Saturday (10.30am) and Thursday (6.30pm) at a cost of $10 per person. Audiotaped tours are available daily: $5 cassette rental.

Gay Beach

🛈 Ocean Drive, Miami Beach | 🕐 7am–midnight | 💲 Free

Flanking famous Ocean Drive is a stretch of sandy beach frequented by gorgeous young gay gentlemen and luscious ladies from Lesbos. The whole beach extends from 5th to 15th Streets, but head for the rainbow flags marking our turf, catch some rays or take a dip in the powerful Atlantic surf while lifeguards watch over you from quaint pastel-coloured huts. You can sunbathe on the sand for free, or beach vendors provide sunbeds at $5 each and shady umbrellas at $10 each. With more muscle per mile than any other beach I've come across, this place lends new meaning to the term 'grilled beef'.

Lincoln Road Mall

🛈 Lincoln Road, Miami Beach

Watch the world go by

Not really a mall, but a picturesque, palmed pedestrianised road that runs from Alton Road to Washington Avenue. Lining it you'll find fashionable clothes stores, health-food shops, art galleries and many gay-friendly bars and restaurants, including gay eatery Balans and late-night gay watering hole Score. An excitingly cosmopolitan mix of people, including cruising muscle boys, heterosexual diners, Haitian street entertainers and vagrants, makes it a great place to people-watch.

Art Deco on Ocean Drive

Ocean Drive

🛈 Miami Beach

Another place to see and be seen. Lined with chic bars, cafés, hotels, shops and restaurants bustling with tourists and locals. The gay beach runs parallel to Ocean Drive so there's always a strong contingent of gay guyz and girlz in evidence. Gay comedy movie *The Birdcage* was filmed at the Carlyle Hotel.

The ornate Versace Mansion that once belonging to murdered gay fashion designer Gianni Versace is further down. Tourists still stop to be photographed on the steps where he was shot by serial killer Andrew Cunanan. During the day, berry-brown rollerbladers streak past in tiny things, while at night cars cruise by.

Venetian Pool

🛈 2701 De Soto Boulevard, Coral Gables, Miami **🕿** 305-460-5356
www.venetianpool.com **🕙** 11am–5.30pm Mon–Fri (except third week Jun–second
week Aug 11am–7.30pm; Nov–Mar 10am–4.30pm); Sat and Sun 10am–4.30pm;
Closed Mon **💲** Nov–Mar $5.50; Apr–Oct $8.50

Bridge of sighs

Built in 1923 from a quarry, Venetian Pool is a stunning aquamarine public swimming hole fed by natural spring water that cascades from waterfalls. Italian-themed, the pool is lined with striped Venetian boat poles and palm trees, studded with coral rock caves, and crossed by a little cobblestone bridge. It even has its own sandy 'beach'. It's all so scenic that many fashion shoots take place here. Movie stars Esther Williams and Johnny 'Tarzan' Weismuller swam here in its heyday, so pop in and experience a slice of life from a bygone age.

Villa Vizcaya

🛈 3251 South Miami Avenue, Miami
🕿 305-250-9133
🕙 9.30am– 4.30pm daily (except Christmas day)
💲 $10

A lavish villa at the edge of Biscayne Bay. This is actually the setting for the annual gay circuit bash The White Party, but well worth a look without all those drunken

Home of The White Party

Muscle Marys cluttering up the place. Built in 1916, but furnished in an overly ornate clash of Italian Renaissance and baroque styles, Villa Vizcaya boasts some stunning and sometimes hideous art and antiques, and ten acres of lavish gardens with enough mazes, fountains and grottoes to explore for hours. Take the free guided tour of the house for a snapshot of the villa's chequered past.

Funky lifeguard hut

Around Town

There's not much of real interest for queer travellers on mainland Miami. But cross the causeways over Biscayne Bay and it's a different story. There you'll find South Beach (SoBe) – the southernmost tip of an island known as Miami Beach. It's in SoBe you'll want to be based during your stay, as almost all the sights, sounds and scene are within walking distance.

South Beach

South Beach, or SoBe to the natives, the southernmost tip of Miami Beach, is by far the gayest district of Miami, and it's easy to see why. Here, the warm winters make socialising *alfresco* possible all year round – everyone makes the most of it with open-air restaurant terraces, pavement sidebars, rollerblading and cycling, as well as frequent strolls down bustling Lincoln Road Mall and the famous Ocean Drive.

Within a few blocks you have a wide, white sandy gay beach, vast and lush Flamingo Park, and some of the prettiest 1930s and 40s art-deco architecture in the world. You also have at your disposal a concentration of restaurants dishing up some of the tastiest cuisine from around the world, a bunch of hip bars and some of the best hotels in all Miami.

Despite the scorching heat, south Florida's humid subtropical climate means that palms, ferns and flowers thrive – sprouting from every possible space and contrasting with the pastel-painted buildings. While the buff and barely-clothed tanned locals whizz by on bicycles or rollerblades, dragonflies flit around and tiny gecko lizards run for cover underfoot. South Beach has all the facilities of a cosmopolitan big city, fused with the leafy, tranquil feel of a small ocean-front suburb.

A DAY OUT

Start the day with a stroll through beautiful Flamingo Park, where you can jog, take a dip in the Olympic-sized open-air pool, or just watch the joggers, cruisers or shirtless guys playing basketball on the practice courts. Then head for a cluster of fashion stores known as the Collins Strip (Collins Avenue between 5th and 8th Streets) to indulge in a little retail

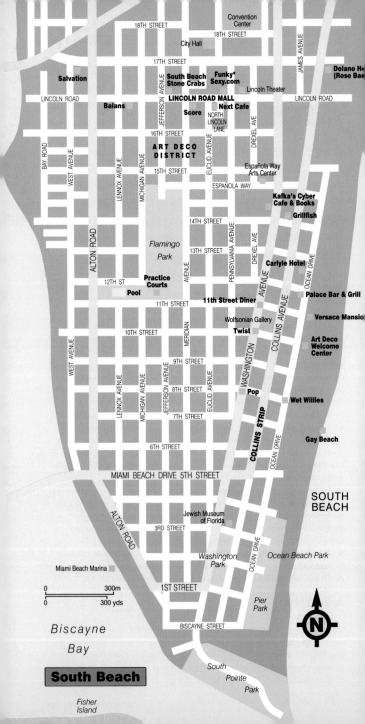

South Beach

18TH STREET
Convention Center
18TH STREET
City Hall
17TH STREET
JAMES AVENUE
Salvation
Delano Ho (Rose Bar
South Beach Stone Crabs
Funky* Sexy.com
JEFFERSON AVENUE
Lincoln Theater
LINCOLN ROAD
LINCOLN ROAD
LINCOLN ROAD MALL
Balans
Score
Next Cafe
NORTH LINCOLN LANE
DREXEL AVE
16TH STREET
ART DECO DISTRICT
EUCLID AVENUE
BAY ROAD
WEST AVENUE
LENNOX AVENUE
MICHIGAN AVENUE
15TH STREET
Española Way Arts Center
ESPAÑOLA WAY
Kafka's Cyber Cafe & Books
Grillfish
14TH STREET
PENNSYLVANIA AVENUE
DREXEL AVE
ALTON ROAD
Flamingo Park
13TH STREET
AVENUE
Carlyle Hotel
OCEAN DRIVE
COLLINS AVENUE
Palace Bar & Grill
Practice Courts
12TH ST
Pool
AVENUE
11TH STREET
11th Street Diner
MERIDIAN
Versace Mansio
Wolfsonian Gallery
Twist
10TH STREET
WASHINGTON
Art Deco Welcome Center
WEST AVENUE
LENNOX AVENUE
MICHIGAN AVENUE
JEFFERSON AVENUE
EUCLID AVENUE
9TH STREET
8TH STREET
Pop
COLLINS STRIP
Wet Willies
7TH STREET
OCEAN DRIVE
6TH STREET
Gay Beach
MIAMI BEACH DRIVE 5TH STREET
SOUTH BEACH
ALTON ROAD
Jewish Museum of Florida
3RD STREET
OCEAN DRIVE
Ocean Beach Park
Washington Park
Miami Beach Marina
0   300m
0   300 yds
1ST STREET
Pier Park
N
Biscayne Bay
BISCAYNE STREET
South Beach
South Pointe Park
Fisher Island

therapy, thanks to the outlets of Armani Exchange, Urban Outfitters, Nike, Speedo, Kenneth Cole and Banana Republic. Next it's on to Ocean Drive to arm yourself with maps, literature and an audiocassette tour from the Art Deco Welcome Center (*see p. 15*). Then work up an appetite exploring the leafy Art Deco District and soaking up some local history from your headset. It's all contained within one square mile, so it's easy to explore at your own pace, or you could take the Welcome Center's 90-minute guided walking tour – for a tour timetable call 305-531-3484.

After lunch, stroll down Ocean Drive. If you are a fan of 1980s cop show *Miami Vice* you'll recognise many sights and sounds. Look out for the Mediterranean-style former Versace Mansion, sold after his death for $23 million, or the Carlyle Hotel, where gay comedy movie *The Birdcage* was filmed. One of the potent frozen cocktails from Wet Willies (*see p. 48*) will knock you out for a while. Take the opportunity to sunbathe at the Lesbian & Gay Beach just opposite gay watering-hole The Palace Bar & Grill at the corner of Ocean Drive and 12th Street. Drench yourself in sunblock and stretch out amongst little art-deco life-saving huts beside the Atlantic Ocean's sandy shores and watch the talent deepening their tans or paddling in the Atlantic surf; whilst being careful not to take in too much sun at once, of course. When you're pink and done to a turn it's time to hit the shops and punish some credit card plastic. There's always fabulous, hip and glittery party clothes to at Pop (*see p. 29*) or Funky*Sexy.com (*see p. 28*).

On your way back to your guest house drop into Kafka's Cyber Cafe and Books (*see p. 28*) to send email messages back home. Back to your room, and after a rest and a change of clothes (wear something relatively smart), stop for cocktails in the amazing lobby bar of the Delano Hotel (*see p. 56*). Then it's on for beer, go-go boys and laughably bad cabaret at Twist (*see p. 46*). While you're there, you can pick up the local free gay listings magazines and decide on exactly which nightclubs to hit.

☕ Out to Lunch

Shelter briefly from the subtropical heat with lunch under the sidewalk umbrellas and palms of the 24-hour **News Cafe**. Late gay fashion designer Gianni Versace ate here regularly and stopped here to buy an Italian newspaper minutes before his assassination on the steps of his nearby mansion in 1997 by gay serial killer Andrew Cunanan. News Cafe is a great place to eat and people-watch, or just bury your head in one of the international newspapers and magazines on sale. Alternatively, try **South Beach Stone Crabs** for seafood pasta, or the **Nexxt Cafe** (*see p. 38*) for mountainous salads.

Light and shade

Mainland Miami

Venture by car across the Venetian, MacArthur or Julia Tuttle causeways that link South Beach to mainland Miami, and life takes on a very different flavour.

Although not nearly as gay as South Beach, Miami is mostly gay-friendly, and there are sights and attractions worth driving across for. Downtown Miami is a built-up business district which becomes almost deserted after 8pm. There isn't a lot to see there, but the surrounding residential districts like pictur-esque Coral Gables and leafy Coconut Grove are worth a peek, and hidden among them are touristy attractions like Parrot Jungle and Gardens (11000 SW 57th Street, tel: 305-666-7834), Monkey Jungle (14805 SW 216th Street, tel: 305-235-1611), Fairchild Tropical Garden (10901 Old Cutler Road, tel: 305-667-1651) and a few architectural surprises like the outrageously grand old Biltmore Hotel (1200 Anastasia Avenue, Coral Gables, tel: 305-445-1926) which actually looks slightly sinister from the outside, like some huge mental asylum. Appropriately enough, Judy Garland used to stay there. Feel free to wander in and take a look and shriek hallelujah, come on and get happy.

A DAY OUT

Take breakfast 1950s-style in the chrome and formica splendour of the bizarre 11th Street Diner (1065 Washington Avenue, Miami Beach). It's an experience in itself and some tasty and cheap greasy-spoon cuisine will set you up for the day's explorations. After breakfast, slowly amble back to your guest house, taking in busy Ocean Drive or Lincoln Road, giving you time to digest your breakfast properly. Pick up your rental car and drive across the scenic Venetian or MacArthur Causeway, high over beautiful Biscayne Bay.

When you reach the mainland, battle through the traffic of Down-town Miami and cruise through residential Coral Gables for a spot of swimming and sunbathing in the astounding make-believe surroundings of the Venetian Pool (*see p. 17*). While you're there, hunt out the wall of black-and-white photographs dating back to the pool's 1920s and 30s heyday for a glimpse at a bygone age of opera performances, 'gypsy' hostesses and bathing beauty contests. The sun's rays are very potent in Florida, so drink plenty of fluids, slap on your sunscreen and sunblock and don't spend too long scorching. Get like the local geckoes and regularly make a break for the shade.

An afternoon tour of Villa Vizcaya (*see p. 17*) will keep you out of the haze for a while. Vizcaya was completed in 1916 by designer Paul Chalfin in homage to 16th-century Italian architecture. As such, it's a laughably lavish clash of mock-Renaissance, rococo and neo-classical

Mainland Miami

DOWNTOWN MIAMI

Cactus (The Prickly Pear)
Lambda Passages Bookstore
Cultural Center
Museum of Southern Florida
BISCAYNE BLVD
BRICKELL AVE
NW 12TH AVE

FINANCIAL DISTRICT

BRICKELL

HAMMOCK

Orange Bowl Stadium
Cuban Museum
SW 3RD AVE
SW 13TH AVE
Museum of Science & Space Transit Planetarium
Villa Vizcaya

NW 7TH STREET
EAST-WEST EXPRESSWAY
WEST FLAGLER STREET
SW 17TH AVENUE
SW 8TH STREET
SW 22ND AVENUE
SW 27TH AVENUE
CORAL WAY

OCEAN VIEW HEIGHTS

Cafe Tu Tu Tango
Miami City Hall
Dinner Key
Marina

Miami Youth Museum
THE PINES
Club Body Center
DOUGLAS ROAD
Coco Walk
GRAND AVE COCONUT GROVE
The Barnacle State Historic Site

Coliseum
SW 42ND AVENUE

Miami International Airport
PONCE DE LEON BLVD
OLD CUTLER ROAD

CORAL GABLES

Venetian Pool
ANASTASIA AVE
DE SOTO BLVD
GRANADA BOULEVARD

Biscayne National Park

University of Miami
Lowe Art Gallery
SW 57TH AVENUE

RED ROAD
Biltmore Hotel
SW 24TH STREET
BIRD ROAD

WEST MIAMI

TAMIAMI TR
SW 67TH AVENUE
Ozone
SW 56TH STREET

SOUTH MIAMI

The Shops at Sunset Place

FLAGLER

Lake Mahar
WEST FLAGLER STREET
DOLPHIN EXPRESSWAY

FLAGAMI

SW 8TH STREET
SW 87TH AVENUE

WESTCHESTER

CORAL WAY
SW 40TH STREET
Blue Lake
MILLER ROAD

PALMETTO EXPRESSWAY

Tropical Park
Lake Catalina
GALLOWAY ROAD
DON SHULA EXPRESSWAY

KENDALL

Monkey Jungle

Biscayne Bay

N

0   1 kilometre
0   1 mile

styles, with more than an air of fairytale about it. Inside you'll find the most extravagant (and sometimes tasteless) art, antiques and antiquities, while the gardens are a fusion of cascading pools, fountains, formal gardens and shady grottoes. It's here that the annual gay circuit bash The White Party takes place each November.

The lavish Villa Vizcaya

If the nearby CocoWalks shops don't appeal, then drive along to the mall at Sunset Place (*see p. 30*). It's far more hip, with a massive Virgin Megastore and many fashion outlets. If you're looking to reaffirm your gaydom, then the Lambda Passages Bookstore (*see p. 34*) is just a short drive away too.

Drive back to Miami Beach to shower and change. Then it's off for dinner. You can dine somewhere nearby. I'd recommend visiting local favourite Grillfish (*see p. 35*) at least once during your stay for their dizzying array of great seafood dishes. By the way, their smoky-tasting grilled lobster is to-die-for. Get there as early as possible to be sure of a table. Alternatively, hop back in the car and make your way back to the mainland for a drink at gay dance bar Cactus (*see p. 47*). They have their own restaurant, The Prickly Pear, so you can grab a bite there too. After 9pm Miami's Latino-flavoured video-bar and dance club the Ozone (*see p. 47*) throws open its doors.

It's actually more fun to bar hop, but be warned, Miami crowds venture out quite late, so it's pretty quiet early on. Then again, if it's a Saturday night you could crank things up a notch or ten by joining the gurning totty waving their hands and shirts in the air at muscle-boy heaven Salvation over at South Beach (*see p. 45*).

If not, then a visit to the cruisey 24-hour Club Body Center (*see p. 51*) gay sauna might really prove to be your salvation.

☕ Out to Lunch

There's a small coffee shop at **Villa Vizcaya** which sells delicious huge gooey cookies, but if you've worked up an appetite, it's better to drive down to **Cafe Tu Tu Tango** (Cocowalk shops, 3015 Grand Avenue, Coconut Grove) for Alligator Bites (fried chunks of breaded alligator) and other tapas-style junk food. There's normally glass painting or some other arts and crafts demonstrations to watch while you're there.

Hey good looking . . .

All Shopped Out

SoBe is a holiday resort catering for both holidaymakers and the region's affluent second homeowners. As such the shopping veers wildly from the trashy to the expensive with little in-between. Drive off to Bal Harbour for designer chic, or Sunset Place mall for mid-range famous name labels. Better still, explore SoBe on foot for its quirky boutiques, audacious club and swimwear, and some, frankly bizarre, giftshops. Browsing these is half the fun.

Top of the Shops

Bal Harbour Mall

ℹ️ 9700 Collins Avenue, Bal Harbour, North Miami Beach ✆ 305-866-0311 www.balharbourshops.com ⏰ 10am–9pm Mon–Fri; 10am–7pm Sat; noon–6pm Sun

You'll need a car or cab to reach Bal Harbour, but you might find it worth the trek to find an upmarket mall crammed with designer outlets from D&G, Gucci, Cartier, Giorgio Armani, Prada, Gap, Chanel, Neimann Marcus and Saks Fifth Avenue, to name but a few. Well worth hunting down is the Art of Shaving (tel: 305-866-0311), an old-style men's grooming emporium and barbershop where you'll be given a close shave that's curiously relaxing despite the cut-throat razors they favour.

Beatnix

ℹ️ 1149 Washington Avenue, Miami Beach. *Washington Avenue: map p.20* ✆ 305-532-8733 ⏰ noon–10pm Mon–Wed; noon–midnight Thu–Sun

Vintage clothing, groovy clubwear, Mardi Gras-style costumes, accessories, exotic wigs, and trashy jewellery and kitsch novelties.
Come by to pick out some cool T-shirts. One particularly camp little number I spotted was emblazoned with the legend: 'Dear Aunt Em, hate you, hate Kansas, took the dog – Dorothy XX'.

Dog Bar

ⓘ 723 North Lincoln Lane, Miami Beach

☎ 305-532-5654

www.dogbar.com

⏰ 10am–10pm daily

Pet's paradise

While you're swanning about on holiday, there's someone pining at home that deserves a treat. Dog Bar is 200 square feet of kitty and pooch worshipping pet superstore. Chic sweaters, coats, zany hats, rainwear and T-shirts, wacky dog bowls, trendy toys and gifts, and groovy sequinned and studded collars that you'll probably want to wear yourself.

The shop is so fascinating that you'll want to buy something even if you don't have a pet.

Funky*Sexy.com

ⓘ 637 Lincoln Road, Miami Beach. See map p. 20

☎ 305-532-2649

email: sfunkysexy@aol.com

⏰ noon–10pm Tues–Sat; noon–8pm Sun and Mon

Outrageous store for men and women carrying hip customised T-shirts, clubwear, combats, leatherwear, second-hand clothing and drag essentials. You never know, one day you might be in the mood for a bright-red Afro wig coordinated with a racy red leather jockstrap!

Kafka's Cybercafe and Books

ⓘ 1464 Washington Avenue, Miami Beach See map p. 20

☎ 305-673-9669

email: kafkascafe@aol.com

⏰ 8.30am–midnight daily

An exhaustive selection of international magazines and books, plus a coffee shop and pay-per-minute internet access. Keep in touch with your friends back home, or just cruise the local chat rooms.

Pop

ⓘ 1151 Washington Avenue, Miami Beach *Washington Avenue: map p. 20*
📞 305-604-9604
www.popsouthbeach.com
🕐 noon–10pm daily

Young, funky clothes and T-shirts for guyz and girlz. Staffed by an entertaining and amiable bunch of young shop assistants and their friends, gay and straight, who entertained themselves (and me) by quizzing customers on whom I most fancied in the shop. Discotastic sparkly tops, clubwear, novelties, gifts and accessories, kitsch nonsense plus terrific second-hand tops and T-shirts.

South Beach Ball

ⓘ 233 12th Street, Miami Beach. *12th Street: map p. 20*
📞 305-532-4100 email: gioball233@aol.com
🕐 11am–7pm Mon–Fri; 11am–9pm Sat; 11am–6pm Sun
💳 Credit cards: AmEx, M, V

Formerly a Tom of Finland store, South Beach Ball has end-of-line stock from the now defunct gay range. and is the only shop I know of that stocks custom-made swim trunks and shorts with an ingenious device to show you off at your best advantage. It special-ises in hats, shirts, combats, surfwear and skimpy swimwear by young US designers.

There's plenty of quirky window shopping in Miami

Sunset Place

ℹ️ 5701 Sunset
Drive, South Miami.
See map p. 24
📞 305-665-4445
www.shopsimon.com
🕐 11am–10pm
Mon–Fri; 11am– 11pm
Sat; 11am–9pm Sun

It's going to be
well worth the
drive to mainland
Miami to find this
funky mall with
an enormous
Virgin
Megastore, and
clothes outlets like

Funky shopping mall

Niketown, Banana Republic, Armani Exchange, Gap and Urban
Outfitters. There's also a large Barnes & Noble bookstore and even an
Imax cinema.

XS Excess

ℹ️ 1652 Collins Avenue, Miami Beach.
Collins Avenue: map p. 20
📞 305-534-4551
🕐 noon–10pm daily

Very reasonable menswear outlet
stocked to the rafters with all the
designer names you could want
including Levi's, DKNY, Guess
and Ralph Lauren. There's some
sexy Sauvage swimwear, cute
Dockers shorts, underwear basics
from Polo and Calvin Klein, and
jeans by Calvin Klein.

Zoo 14

ℹ️ 933 Washington Avenue, Miami
Beach. *Washington Avenue: map p.20*
📞 305-538-4273 email:
zoo14florida@aol.com
🕐 noon 8pm Mon–Sat; noon–5pm Sun

Menswear, Gregg Homme
underwear, swim trunks $32,
discotastic clubwear. You'll be lost
without blinding wardrobe
essentials like their silver-sequinned
trousers $58, or black-tassel trousers
$95, topped off with one of their
leopard-print cowboy hats.

Ready for action at Zoo 14

Shop Around

To show off your figure

BODY BODY WEAR
943 Washington Avenue, Miami Beach
305-531-6325
www.bodybodywear.com
noon–8pm Mon–Thu; noon–9pm Fri & Sat; noon–7pm Sun

Tight and sexy body-hugging swimwear- and clubwear designed by Stephen Sandler. Shirts, underwear, T-shirts, vests, shorts and trousers. Pop in to find something for the muscle man in your life.

LAMBDA PASSAGES BOOKSTORE
7545 Biscayne Boulevard, Miami
305-754-6900
noon–10pm daily

A smallish selection of gay and lesbian books and magazines, plus masses of adult gay videos, Gay Pride flags, lube, toys, etc.

PLEASURE EMPORIUM
1671A Alton Road & 1019 5th Street, Miami Beach

305-538-6434
24 hours daily

Mixed gay/straight sex shop stocking a large selection of magazines and videos and a small selection of toys, lube, harnesses, condoms, fetishwear and novelties.

POST BLUE JEAN CO
836 Lincoln Road, Miami Beach
305-673-2124
noon–11pm daily

The place to pick up the most fashionable denims in SoBe. Stocks all the biggest labels including Levi's, DKNY, Calvin Klein and some nice little numbers from Diesel.

SOURCE PARIS
728 Lincoln Road, Miami Beach
305-672-2675
11am–11.30pm Mon–Thu; 11am–midnight Fri & Sat; 11am–11pm Sun

Stylish European menswear on two levels. Kit yourself out in shoes, trousers and denim jeans. There's a great line in linen-wear for those who enjoy ironing a lot, plus a womenswear concession a couple of doors down (718 Lincoln Road).

SPEC'S MUSIC AND VIDEO

🛈 501 Collins Avenue, Miami Beach
☎ 305-534-3667
🕐 noon–10pm daily

Just off the beaten track, a massive two-floor emporium packed with new and hard-to-find oldies on CD. Upstairs has a terrific DVD section, especially for horror buffs, with extensive sections for classic musicals, thrillers, comedy and music promos.

WATCH THIS OPTICAL

🛈 521 Lincoln Road, Miami Beach
☎ 305-538-9350
🕐 noon–10pm Mon–Thu; noon–11pm Fri and Sat; noon–10pm Sun

Huge selection of designer sun-glasses – you're gonna need them here – from Versace, Guess, Moschino, Gucci, Cartier, Ralph Lauren Polo, Armani, Persol, Ray-Ban, Chanel, Kenneth Cole, Revo, Web and Dolce & Gabbana.

WHITTALL AND SHON

🛈 1319 Washington Avenue, Miami Beach
☎ 305-538-2606
www.whittallshon.com
🕐 noon–10pm daily

Loud and lewd men's club-, gym-and swim-wear. If you like it sheer or shiny, this is the store for you. PVC cop shirts, snakeskin-print jeans, tie-dye vests, gold PVC trousers, sleeveless T-shirts and bright swim trunks are among those flashy body-skimming designs that gay men lap up.

Cowboy kitsch

Authentic American diner

Eating Out

Hungry? You've come to the right place. SoBe has some of the best, swankest, and most diverse dinning in all of South Florida. Seafood, exotic salads, traditional American, Caribbean, Italian, Mexican... take your pick. And here you can romance alfresco under a blanket of twinkling stars, pig out on some of the tastiest cheap eats around, or head for the latest hotspot to rub shoulders with the rich and famished.

Cream of the Cuisine

11th Street Diner

🛈 1065 Washington Avenue and 11th Street, Miami Beach. *See map p. 20* 🌐 305-534-6373 🕒 noon–midnight Mon–Thu and Sun; 24 hours Fri Sat 🍴 🍽 – 🍽

Authentic 50s-style diner and bar decked out in retro chrome and formica with shiny red vinyl seats, booths and bar stools to perch at the counter. Filling American greasy-spoon cuisine awaits. Try their enormous Everything Burger, wash it down with a traditional Amber Rock beer and contemplate the cake stand if you dare.

Flame grilled

Grillfish

🛈 1444 Collins Avenue, Miami Beach. *See map p. 20*
🌐 305-538-9908 🕒 6pm–midnight daily
🍴 🍽 – 🍽

Bustling gay-friendly seafood restaurant, and a favourite of the locals. Dine by the light of Gothic chandeliers beneath a huge Renaissance-style mural. Great food, prompt service and the open kitchen so you can watch the chefs flambé your food. I recommend the spiced clams or smoky-flavoured lobster, which was the best I've ever had.

> **The following price guides have been used for eating out and indicate the price for a main course:**
>
> 🍽 = **cheap** = under $10
>
> 🍽 = **moderate** = $10–$20
>
> 🍽 = **expensive** = over $20

Front Porch Cafe

ⓘ Penguin Hotel,
1418 Ocean Drive,
Miami Beach. *Ocean Drive:
map p. 20*
📞 305-534-9334
www.penguinhotel.com
🕑 8am–10.30pm
daily **🍴 🍽 – 🍽**

Cheapish breakfast,
lunch and dinner
served on a terrace
overlooking Ocean
Drive, and a quick
stroll from the Gay

Dine out on Ocean Drive

Beach. Here you must try the three salad sampler which lets you mix
your own selection of different salads for $9.95. I recommend combining
the tuna, curry chicken and artichoke salads. Portions are big and prices
reasonable. Watch the world and his wife (or homosexual lover) pass by
on Ocean Drive and drink in a soundtrack of retro classics from the likes
of Culture Club and Dead Or Alive.

Sophisicated suppering

Liaison Restaurant & Bar

ⓘ 1436 Drexel Avenue,
Miami Beach. Drexel
Avenue: map p. 20
📞 305-538-1055
www.liaisonrestaurant.com
🕑 6pm–midnight
Mon–Sat; 11am–3pm,
6pm–midnight Sun
🍴 🍽 – 🍽

Quite a find, this gay-
friendly husband-
and-wife run bar

and restaurant boasts quality food and a sophisticated ambience at very
affordable prices. Featuring a New Orleans-French fusion and a menu
which changes daily and offers delicacies like Louisiana redfish, barbecue
shrimp, tangy turtle soup and homemade sorbets. An ideal place to take
a loved one for a romantic meal.

Moonlight Caffe/Oh Mexico

Have a margarita in Oh Mexico

1440 Washington Avenue, Miami Beach. *Washington Avenue: map p. 20*

305-532-0490

7am–1am daily

A real find, just far enough away from the main drag to be guaranteed a table. Serving a range of Italian and Mexican cuisine, with an extensive variety of margarita cocktails to wash it all down. Portions are big, service is quick and friendly, and on Friday nights there's a sleepy little local arts and crafts market on Espanalo Way right outside.

News Cafe

800 Ocean Drive, Miami Beach. *Ocean Drive: map p. 20*

305-538-6397

www.newscafe.com

24 hours daily

A Versace favourite

Indoor/outdoor sidewalk restaurant that was a favourite with the late fashion designer Gianni Versace. Inside you can buy international newspapers and magazines, which makes it a great place to hang out. Order terrific breakfasts, fruit plates, calamari, chicken, salmon and pecan salads, Middle-Eastern snacks, pastas and juices. Always busy and bustling with activity, and open 24 hours.

Nexxt Cafe

700 Lincoln Road, Miami
Beach. *See map p. 20*

305-532-6643

11am–11pm Sun–Thu;
11am-midnight
Fri and Sat

Time to eat

Despite the huge outside
sidewalk terrace and
sizeable two-tier interior,
there's usually a bit of a
wait until you get your
paws on the Nexxt's simple but quality European-American hybrid
cuisine. Expect pasta, burgers, seafood and pizza given a flavourful spin.
Register your name at the door and put up with those tummy rumbles.
It's worth it. Popular dishes include Jambalaya Pasta, Chinese Salad,
Popcorn Shrimp and Crab & Avocado Roll. But order one of their
enormous Border Salads just once and you'll be back. Great French
pastries and frozen margaritas too.

Alfresco eating at Nexxt Cafe

Grillfish – flaming seafood

South Beach Stone Crabs

ℹ 927 Lincoln Road, Miami Beach. *See map p. 20*

🌐 305-538-5888 | ⏰ noon–11pm Mon–Thu and Sun; noon–midnight Fri and Sat | 🍴 💳 – 💳

Head here for great mounds of seafood pasta heavy with prawns, fish and scallops, which is also one of the cheaper options. Stone crab claws are a speciality here, but more expensive. Situated in the middle of pedestrianised Lincoln Road amid dense palms and lanterns, this place has a great ambience to it. Gay-friendly.

Spiga

ℹ Hotel Impala,1228 Collins Avenue, *Collins Avenue: map p. 20* | 🌐 305-534-0079 www.spigarestaurant.com

⏰ 6–11pm Sun–Thu; 6pm–midnight Fri and Sat | 🍴 💳 – 💳

Recommended by locals, this hotel restaurant is open to all and has a big local gay following, so arrive early to bag a table in the open air. Drop by forsucculent Italian cuisine, filling spinach or shrimp salads, seafood soups, grilled fish or chicken and, of course, rich ravioli, linguine, tagliatelle and fettuccine pasta heavy with cherry tomatoes, balsamic vinegar, seafood or sautéed chicken and dripping with tomato sauces, ricotta or cream. Not perhaps the place for dieters.

Best of the Rest

BAL HARBOUR

CARPACCIO

 Bal Harbour Shops, 9700 Collins Avenue, North Miami Beach 305-867-7777 11.30am–11pm daily

Enjoy delicious but pricey Italian cuisine alongside the Ladies Who Lunch at this eatery in an exclusive tropical oasis designer shopping mall. Dine on the palmed out-door terrace if you want to spy on the affluent ladies and their pampered pooches doing some serious damage to their husbands' platinum credit cards.

COCONUT GROVE

CAFE TU TU TANGO

 Cocowalk, 3015 Grand Avenue, Coconut Grove 305-529-2222 www.cafetututango.com 11.30am–2am Fri and Sat; 11.30am– midnight Sun–Wed; 11.30am–1am Thu

Bohemian two-level themed restaurant decked out like an artist's garret. The menu looks like an artist's palette, the cutlery is served in a mixing jar, there are live arts and crafts demonstrations throughout the day, and a popular sun-drenched outdoor terrace. Food is of the quick-fix fast-food variety and is served in tapas-like portions for you to pick at as you drink in the ambience.

MIAMI BEACH

BALANS

 1022 Lincoln Road, Miami Beach 305-534-9191 8am–midnight Sun– Thu; 8am–1am Fri and Sat

Florida franchise of the London-based gay restaurant chain serving a similarly limited menu with a slightly pretentious modern-European flair. Decent food, reasonable portions. Burgers and breakfasts are a safe bet, even the most common foods are dressed up with elaborate trimmings to make them seem a little bit special.

B.E.D.

 929 Washington Avenue, Miami Beach 305-532-9070 8pm–midnight daily

Novelty costs, and while dining cross-legged on the huge Bedouin-style beds might seem like a blast, B.E.D.'s successful à la carte fusion of French, Mediterranean and Asian cuisine is a little pricey. That doesn't seem to deter SoBe's thrill-seeking diners though, and as there are only two seatings a night, and same-day reservations only, you'll need to book first thing.

FAIRWIND CAFE
ℹ️ 1000 Collins Avenue, Miami Beach
📞 305-531-0050
🕐 7.30am–midnight daily
🍴 🏧

Caribbean-style fast-food cuisine in a large, lush, tropical garden setting off busy Collins Avenue, not far from the Gay Beach. A great place for snacks and even better for elaborate early evening cocktails.

GRILLSTEAK
ℹ️ 1438 Collins Avenue, Miami Beach
📞 305-538-9908
www.grillfish.com
🕐 6pm–midnight daily
🍴 🏧 – 🏧

Carnivore heaven – demolish large portions of grilled beef, pork, lamb and chicken, in the form of steaks, kebabs, sausages, salads and *burritos*. Steaks come with a choice of Mushrooms in Port-Wine, Horseradish Cream or Raspberry Vinaigrette. Housed in a cosy rustic setting styled on an old Tuscan basement kitchen. Older sister Grillfish is next door.

PALACE BAR AND GRILL
ℹ️ 1200 Ocean Drive, Miami Beach
📞 305-531-9077
🕐 8am–midnight daily
🍴 🏧

Gay terrace restaurant right across the street from the 12th Street gay beach. The menu of burgers, salads and sandwiches may be simple and unfussy, but it's a great place for people-watching and somewhere shady to take a breather from all that sun worshipping.

POLLO TROPICAL
ℹ️ 1454 Alton Road, Miami Beach
📞 866-769-7696
www.go2pollotropical.com
🕐 8am–midnight daily
🍴 🏧

The place for cheap but tasty food in a hurry, this Caribbean-flavoured fast-food joint dishes up flame-grilled chicken, shrimp and pork dishes, usually served with black beans and white rice. There's also some great Caesar salads on the menu, fries come French- or Yucatan-style, and desserts are sticky and sweet Key Lime Pie, Flan or gooey Caribbean Creme Cake.

Cocktail time at Fairwind Cafe

Out on the Town

SoBe is Circuit Party central, and most clubs and bars here cater for the shirts-in-the-air muscle boys who frequent 'em each season. Pumped-up pectorals are the look du jour, and pulsing tribal and house the local groove. Salvation, Anthem and Federation are great examples of SoBe's hedonistic machismo, but, if you're looking for a slower pace and a less ecstatic crowd, then try the low-key cabaret/disco/go-go bar delights of Twist, go see and be seen at the Delano's posh Rose Bar, or join the Levi's and leather crowd at the Loading Zone.

My Top Clubs

Keep an eye out for party nights

Anthem at the CroBar

ℹ️ Cameo Theatre, 1445 Washington Avenue, Miami Beach. *Washington Avenue: map p. 20*

📞 305-531-8225
www.crobarmiami.com
🕙 10pm–5am Mon–Thu; 10pm–5am Sun
💲 $15 Mon; $20 Thu and Sun; $25 Fri and Sat

Sunday's queerfest Anthem is the best night at the CroBar. With a soundtrack of classic gay anthems and one of the most diverse dance- club crowds in SoBe, it's less intimidating than some of the muscle-boy strongholds. The gallery levels give you plenty of places to run around or watch the dance-floor movers and shakers, drag divas and go-go boys. Throughout the week there's a parade of other nights, spinning everything from progressive house and disco to funk, soul, hip hop and r'n'b. Call ahead for the latest nightly line-up. Dress casual, designer or drag for the diverse 20s and 30s crowd.

Beauty Bar

ℹ️ Albion Hotel, 1650 James Avenue, Miami Beach. *James Avenue: map p. 20*
📞 305-374-9019
🌐 www.beautybar.com
🕐 5pm–4am Mon–Fri; 7pm–4am Sat and Sun
💲 Free

Fashionable mixed gay/straight hotel bar, but well worth a visit for its sheer quirkiness. Done out like a 1950s beauty salon, complete with an authentic smell of perming lotion, vintage hairdryers, beauty products and old advertisements. Themed cocktails served by the bartending Beauty School Drop-Outs mean you can order a Perm, Platinum Blonde, French Flip, or perhaps a glass of Shampoo (josé cuervo, sweet & sour, triple sec, lime juice & chambord). Part of a chain which includes outlets in New York and LA, Beauty Bar has featured in TV's *Sex and the City*. Happy hour 6–9pm Thursday. Dress designer; 30s–50s locals and hotel residents' crowd.

Federation at Level

ℹ️ 1235 Washington Avenue, Miami Beach 📞 305-532-1525 www.levelnightclub.com
🕐 10pm–5am Fri 💲 Free before 11pm, $20 after

Essential weekly gay night at this huge complex once owned by Prince. Today it's peopled by gurning shirtless muscle boys, drag queens and go-go dancers. Gets busy about 1am, but arrive early for the free admission and free drinks 10–11pm. Although Friday is official gay night, Level is open Wednesday to Monday with other straight but gay-friendly nights. Check the website for details. Dress drag, labels, or shirtless if you've got muscles, for the 20s and 30s crowd.

Laundry Bar

ℹ️ 721 North Lincoln Lane, Miami Beach 📞 305-531-7700 🕐 noon–5am daily 💲 Free

More themed Miami madness. This place has a working launderette in it, so you can wash your smalls as you drink, play pool or sit up at the bar watching music videos and enjoying the charmingly pungent aroma of laundry detergent. Attracts a gay-friendly mixed casual crowd, and, I suppose, lots of people with compulsive disorders relating to cleanliness. Dress casual; 20s and 30s crowd.

Shirts optional

Loading Zone

ℹ 1426A Alton Road, Miami Beach.
Alton Road: map p. 20 **☏** 305-531-LOAD
🕐 10pm–5am daily **💲** Free

Hidden in an alleyway behind
Domino's Pizza and Subway is
SoBe's only leather-and-Levi's bar.
Head here well after midnight,
because this place gets going late.
Inside it's industrial chic, with pool
table, porn screens and Dr Who
pinball machine. There's a smaller
back bar which also sells a small
range of fetish gear. Stay awake till
3am to see it at its cruisiest. There's
no dress code, except on Thursdays
when you have to dress in leather,
or else take your shirt off. Most go
for the topless option. Dress casual
but butch; 20s–50s crowd.

Salvation

ℹ 1771 West Avenue, Miami. *See map
p. 20* **☏** 305-673-6508
www.salvationsobe.com
🕐 10pm–5am Sat; 8am–late Sun
💲 Free before 11pm, $25 after

Check your mind and shirt at the
door, and join the topless gurning
muscle boys at this massive and
male-dominated gay dance club.
Inside its warehouse-like expanses
there's an enormous dance floor,
overlooked by a balcony, and a
chill-out sofa space. There's so
much posing, cruising and muscle
mania you can almost smell the
testosterone in the air, or
was it just the poppers? Casual or
designer shorts/trousers; largely
topless, 20s and 30s crowd.

At the Loading Zone

Twist

🛈 1057 Washington Avenue, Miami
Beach. *Washington Avenue: map p. 20*
📞 305-53-TWIST www.twistsobe.com
🕐 1pm–5am daily 🎟 Free

Very popular multi-roomed bar.
Definitely one to visit earlier in
the evening. Inside you'll find a
narrow ground-floor bar screening
videos; upstairs there's a cruisey
circular bar and tiny dance floor;
round the corner there's a narrow
cabaret bar which features regular
mimed drag shows from the
resident artistes. At the back there's
a quieter bar, and steps leading to
the outside Bungalow Bar, which
barely contains over-friendly go-
go boys daring you to stuff dollars
down their jocks. Dress casual; age
range 20s–50s.

Rose Bar
at the Delano

🛈 Delano Hotel, 1685 Collins Avenue,
Miami Beach. *See map p. 20*
📞 305-672-2000
🕐 noon–2am daily 🎟 Free

Head here for sophisticated early-
evening cocktails amid a frisky
but dressy young gay-friendly
crowd of chic locals and moneyed
hotel residents, all enjoying the
ambience of the Delano's
luxurious Phillipe Starck-designed
lobby, surrealist garden and magical
poolside. No glass allowed around
the pool, but there are staff on-
hand with plastic containers into
which to transfer your cocktails.
Mixed gay/straight. Dress smart
and chic; 20s–50s crowd of hip
locals and hotel residents.

Miami – lively clubs, packed dancefloors

A potent force

BOARDWALK

ℹ️ 17008 Collins Avenue, North Miami Beach

📞 305-949-4119

🕐 6am–5am daily

💲 Free before 10pm, then $5 for men and $10 for women

Look at the prices and guess which gender of clientele they're trying to discourage! A long-running male revue club which was closed for ages but relaunched last year. Live male strippers (6–10pm) plus drag and go-go boys. Raunchy shows take place daily (main show at 10.30pm). Situated a long, long way down Collins Avenue, well away from the SoBe circuit, so be prepared to drive. Dress casual 20s–50s crowd.

CACTUS

ℹ️ 2041 Biscayne Boulevard, Miami

📞 305-438-0662

www.thecactus.com

🕐 3pm–3am Mon–Sat; noon–3am Sun

💲 Free

Mainland gay dance bar with adjacent restaurant, The Prickly Pear. The energetic mix of salsa, merengue and house music makes this place popular with both the SoBe crowd and local Latino boys alike. Inside are two video bars and a games room done out with kitsch Western-style decor. Best night is Friday. Casual SoBe and Latino crowd, in their 20s and 30s.

Live music

OZONE

ℹ️ 6620 SW 57th Avenue, Miami

📞 305-667-2888

🕐 9pm–5am daily

💲 Free to members all night, non-members free before 11pm then $5 for guys and $10 for women

Labyrinth-like warehouse space featuring several spaces including a video bar, lounge and sizeable dance floor. Very popular with the young Latino set, attracted by the Latin house, salsa and drag nights. 21s and over

All Clubbed Out

only. Casual SoBe and Latino lovers crowd, in their 20s and 30s.

SCORE

ℹ 727 Lincoln Road & Meridian Avenue, Miami Beach

☎ 305-535-1111
www.scorebar.com

⏰ 3pm–5am daily

🎟 Free

Large, two-room cabaret bar meets dance club right in the heart of busy Lincoln Road. Busy late, due to the late licence. The weekly line-up includes cabaret and muscly go-go boys. Popular nights include Wednesday's amateur male strip session (10.30pm) and Sunday's tea dance (from 6pm). Pop in to the bar after dining nearby. Dress casual; 30s and 40s crowd.

WET WILLIES

ℹ Ocean Drive & 8th Street, Miami Beach

☎ 305-532-5650

⏰ 11am–2am Sun–Thu; 11am–3am Fri & Sat

🎟 Free

Perhaps the one place in SoBe where you can have sex on the beach legally! This, and other mind-meldingly potent cocktails, are all deceptively frozen into an innocuous-looking Slush Puppy-type concoction, the brute strength of which will take you by surprise. Think you're tough enough? Take my advice, order some calamari to accompany it, stick to one cocktail per person, and watch that traffic when you cross the street. Mixed gay/straight. Dress beach casual; 20s and 30s crowd.

Late night venue

Festivals and Annual Parties

WINTER PARTY
MARCH
www.winterparty.com
Annual fund-raising weekend
in aid of the Dade Human
Rights Foundation Community
Grants Program which funds
a variety of local lesbian,
gay and transgender
organisations. Culminates with
the Official Winter Party on
South Miami Beach at 14th
Street and Ocean Drive.

Pump up the volume

MIAMI GAY & LESBIAN FILM FESTIVAL
APRIL
www.miamigaylesbianfilm.com
Annual festival of lesbian and gay film, documentary and shorts
held at the Colony Theater, a popular cinema complex at the top
of Lincoln Road, Miami Beach.

AQUA GIRL
MAY
www.aquagirl.org
Lesbian-
orientated annual
week of women's
charity club and
social events in
aid of the Dade
Human Rights
Foundation
Women's Fund.

WHITE PARTY WEEK
NOVEMBER

The white house for a White Party

www.whiteparty.net
Six days and nights of testosterone-fuelled partying, raising
money to fight HIV/AIDS. Takes place at various venues around
Miami Beach, culminating with The White Party at Villa Vizcaya on
the Miami mainland.

Say hello to a healthy drink

Working Out

With a preponderance of healthy food and outdoor living, it's easy to be healthy in Miami, and the gorgeous locals might inspire you to start shaping up. Gyms are plenty here, but in keeping with the alfresco feel you might just want to jog along the beach, shoot some baskets in Flamingo Park, or redress some of the damage you've done out on the town by fortifying yourself with leisurely walks and health eats. You're on holiday - why sweat it?!

OUTLINES

BEAUTY DUNGEON

🛈 Private central Miami Beach location. Address given with appointment time

📞 305-534-3484

🕐 24 hours daily

Professional gay service offering haircuts, waxing, facials, body hair removal and massage done conventional style or in Master Paolo's Dungeon.

CAFE BONJOUR

🛈 865 Collins Avenue, Miami Beach

📞 305-673-3668

🕐 7am–2am daily

💳 Credit cards

Papaya, mango, banana and peach tropical smoothies blended with honey and ice ($3.45–$3.95). Fruit salad ($3.50–$4.95). Vegetable juices in celery, cucumber, parsley, carrot, beets, apple and tomato ($4.95).

CLUB BODY CENTER

🛈 2991 Coral Way, Miami

📞 305-448-2214

www.clubbodycenter.com

email: cbcmiami@aol.com

🕐 24 hours daily

Gay sauna over on mainland Miami. Mr Nude Miami Contests, video lounge, drinks and BBQ, plus weekly porn star shows from the likes of Bobby Blake and Flex Dion.

FLAMINGO PARK

🛈 Between Michigan & Meridian Avenues and 11th and 15th Streets, Miami Beach

🕐 5am–midnight daily

Bikes on the beach

Leafy public park which is popular day and night with local gay men. Facilities include clay tennis courts, basketball courts, running track, baseball, squash courts plus a newly rebuilt Olympic-sized public swimming pool with busy men's room opposite. Frequently patrolled by police at night, after complaints by residents, due to its popularity with gay men.

You too can have a figure like this

GNC (GENERAL NUTRITION CENTER)

ℹ️ 622 Lincoln Road, Miami Beach 📞 305-532-2513 🕐 noon–10pm daily

Health-food outlet stocking natural health- food products, diet supplements, protein bars, fat metabolisers, herbal remedies, weight gain

It does you good

In case you are too tired to walk

and weight loss pills, health books, ab slides, and other healthy stuff designed to provide your well-deserved holiday indulgences. While you're there, check out their touchscreen computer guide to nutrition for tips on eating right.

GOLD'S GYM
🛈 1400 Alton Road, Miami Beach
📞 305-538-4653
www.goldsgym.com/southbeach
🕐 5am–midnight Mon–Fri; 7am–11pm Sat; 8am–10pm Sun
💳 Daily passes $20; weekly passes $74.55

Impressive new multi-level gym complex, popular with the local muscle queens. Inside are three floors of fitness including tanning, juice bar, sportswear shop, sundecks, free weights, aerobics, kick boxing and rooftop gym. One of the sundecks is clothing-optional. Situated near the Loading Zone club, just a short walk from South Beach Villas guest house.

WILD OATS COMMUNITY MARKET
🛈 1020 Alton Road, Miami Beach
📞 305-532-1707
🕐 8am–11pm daily

Health nut paradise with aisle upon aisle of natural groceries, organic produce, vitamins, supplements and bodycare products. Check out their great salad bar, fresh fruit and *sushi* lunchboxes, if you're looking for a cheap tasty lunch on a health trip. Browse their extensive range of suncreams, sunblock and after-sun skin treatments with vitamin E and aloe vera if you've been tanning your hide.

Picture yourself lounging by the Jefferson's pool

Checking In

Deep pockets can bring you the luxury of the arty Delano or grand Shelborne hotel, but you might prefer to stay among the immaculate home-from-home comforts on offer at The Jefferson, sample the swish modernity of The Townhouse, or make some new friends at the ever congenial (and sometimes rather saucy) South Beach Villas. When it comes to crashing out, South Beach definitely has something to suit everyone...

The Best Beds

Bohemia

ℹ 825 Michigan Avenue, Miami Beach. *Michigan Avenue: map p. 20*
📞 305-534-1322 email: bohemiahouse@aol.com www.bohemia825.com
🍽 ❷

The following price guides have been used for accommodation, per room per night :

❶ = cheap = under $75

❷ = moderate = $75 – $200

❸ = expensive = $200 and over

A new gay-men-only guest house in the heart of the Art Deco District. Although there's no swimming pool, the grounds are a secluded tropical garden, clothing is optional and there is a jacuzzi. No smoking.

Brigham Gardens

ℹ 1411 Collins Avenue, Miami Beach. *Collins Avenue: map p. 20* 📞 305-531-1331 email: brighamg@ bellsouth.net www.brighamgardens.com Fax: 305-538-9898
🍽 ❷

Lush Caribbean-style family-run guest house right in the heart of everything, set in a beautiful tropical garden complete with fountain and aviary. Mixed gay and straight.

Delano

 1685 Collins Avenue,
Miami Beach. *See map p. 20*

305-672-2000
email: delano@ianschragerhotels.com
Fax: 305-532-0099

America's coolest hotel

Designed by Phillippe Starck –
with a restaurant, the Blue Door,
once owned by Madonna – Ian
Schrager's Delano Hotel is,
according to *Vogue*: 'America's coolest hotel'. Rows of billowing white
drapes, monochrome white rooms and a surreal garden featuring a
perpetually overflowing swimming pool, and stocked with iron
bedsteads, standard lamps sprouting from the grass, tables set with lit
candelabra, a giant chess set and seats cut from the hedgerows give the
place a sort of *Alice in Wonderland* meets psychiatric hospital feel. Mixed
gay and straight.

A gay favourite

Jefferson House

 1018 Jefferson Avenue, Miami Beach. *Jefferson House: map p. 20* 305-534-5247 email:stay@thejeffersonhouse.com www.jeffersonhouse.com Fax: 305-534-5953

Coral-pink, gay-owned art-deco bed and breakfast just half a block from cruisey Flamingo Park and, like most accommodation here, within walking distance of the Gay Beach, shopping, restaurants and nightlife a few blocks away. Homely rather than cruisey, with communal lounge with wide-screen TV, free use of computer with internet access and free video library; light, two-course gourmet breakfast included. Palm-lined sundeck with splash pool and sun loungers. Free coffee bar and newspapers. Air-conditioned rooms contain cable TV/video, CD player. Some with bathrooms en suite. One of the best. Mixed gay and lesbian.

The Shelborne

 1801 Collins Avenue, Miami Beach. *Collins Avenue: map p. 20* 305-531-1271 www.shelborne.com Fax: 305-531-2206

Huge, gay-friendly ocean-front resort with private beach right on the Atlantic. The overblown Art-Deco grandeur gives this

Splash out at the Shelborne

grand hotel a feel of The Overlook Hotel from the movie *The Shining* – in the nicest possible sense. This, the stunning views of the Atlantic, and the proximity to Lincoln Road make it worth splashing out for. Mixed gay and straight.

South Beach Villas

 1201 West Avenue, Miami Beach. *West Avenue: map p. 20* 305-673-9600 email: sobevillas@aol.com www.southbeachvillas.com Fax: 305-532-6200

The friendly atmosphere of this gay-owned and run resort makes it an ideal place to stay, especially if you're travelling alone. Rooms with cable TV and video, clothing-optional swimming pool and outdoor jacuzzi. Communal Continental breakfast and the free poolside margaritas, wine and snacks nightly are a great opportunity to meet other guests. One of the best. Mixed gay and lesbian.

Townhouse

 150 20th Street, Miami Beach 305-534-3800 email: info@townhousehotel.com www.townhousehotel.com Fax: 305-534-3811

State-of-the-art.

Sleeping Around

MIAMI BEACH

BAYLISS GUEST HOUSE

 504 14th Street, Miami Beach 305-531-3755

Small, gay-friendly art-deco hotel. Rooms are spacious despite the cheap rates, and it's well within walking distance of the Loading Zone, Flamingo Park and the bars and restaurants of Lincoln Road. Rooms come with cable TV and there's laundry – always handy.

BEACHCOMBER

1340 Collins Avenue, Miami Beach

305-531-3755

email: beachcomber@travelbase.com

www.beachcomber miami.com

Fax: 305-673-8609

Small but very chic gay-friendly hotel with its own bar and bistro. Art deco in style, Beachcomber is particularly close to Ocean Drive and the designer fashion boutiques of the Collins Strip.

COLOURS INTERNATIONAL

255 West 24th Street, Miami Beach

305-532-9341

email: newcolours@aol.com

www.colours.net

Gay-owned gay and lesbian studios with swimming pool and gym. A little off the main drag, Colours is within walking distance of Lincoln

South Beach Villas

It's Lily's sister

Road, but also just a short cab ride from some of the bars and the gay beach at 12th Street.

HOTEL SHELLEY

 844 Collins Avenue, Miami Beach

305-531-3341

www.southbeachgroup.com

email: Info@southbeach group.com

Sympathetically renovated 30s art-deco hotel. A sister to the nearby Lily Guest House and similarly close to Ocean Drive, the gay beach and

Twist nightclub. Satellite TV, newly decorated deco-style rooms, bar and lounge. Gay-friendly.

LILY GUEST HOUSE

 835 Collins Avenue, Miami Beach

305-535-9900

www.southbeachgroup.com

email: Info@southbeach group.com

Sister place to Hotel Shelley and similarly well maintained. Wood floors, tropical decor, cable TV and private sundeck for guests. Half a block

from Ocean Drive, and close to the Gay Beach and Twist night-club. Gay-friendly.

NORMANDY SOUTH

2474 Prairie Avenue, Miami Beach

305-674-1197

www.normandysouth.com

Go nude anywhere in this clothing-optional men-only guest house close to the Art Deco District. Gay run and owned, Normandy South boasts a swimming pool and outdoor hot tub. No smoking throughout.

DANGER
HAZARDO
CONDI

International rescue

Fort Lauderdale

Thanks to 1960s Fort Lauderdale-based teen flick *Where The Boys Are*, throughout the 1960s, 70s and 80s Fort Lauderdale was regularly besieged by rowdy college kids on their spring break. The drunken antics of those naughty tykes caused so much trouble that 12 years ago they were ousted, and so began a regeneration which is still taking place today.

In 2000 around 670,000 gay and lesbian travellers dropped by for a visit. Yet, until now, word about Fort Lauderdale's gay appeal has yet to spread outside the US. That's all about to change, with a tourist board actively rolling out the rainbow carpet with publicity campaigns designed to target the international pink pound.

Fort Lauderdale combines a thriving gay scene with a flavour of real motor-city America. Very built-up, it isn't as pretty as Key West or Miami Beach, although there are neighbourhoods that are picturesque, like East Las Olas shopping strip, and the palm-lined beach district which boasts many renovated orange, pink and turquoise 1950s motels and guest houses. The more upmarket homes nestling in a network of pretty canals around other parts of Las Olas Boulevard have gained Fort Lauderdale the reputation of being the Venice of America.

The Venice of America

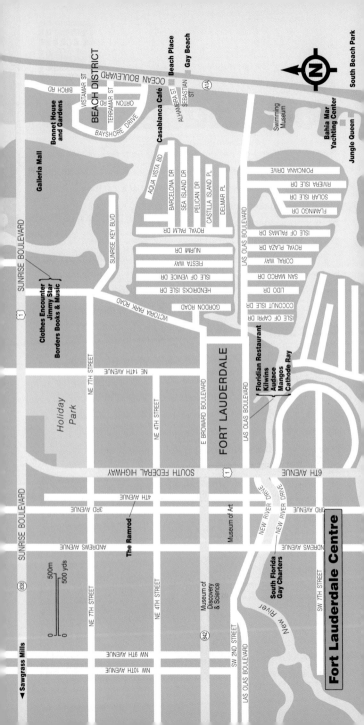

Fort Lauderdale Centre

Here the locals are friendlier than the body-fascists of Miami Beach and the scene is far more diverse, with a strong leather scene. Fort Lauderdale has 23 miles of sandy beaches, around two dozen gay bars, dance and leather clubs, more than 40 gay-friendly shops and restaurants, and over 20 gay guest houses and resorts, the best of which are detailed below.

It's hard to get a sense of scale from guides and maps, but, unlike Miami Beach and Key West, both of which can largely be navigated on foot, Fort Lauderdale is a vast place designed for the motor car. Public transport is somewhat lacking, so unless you drive or can afford numerous cab trips, it can be frustrating. You'll really need to hire a car, or befriend some generous locals. If you do plan to rely on cabs, pick your accommodation carefully. You'll want to stay as close as possible to the bars, restaurants and clubs you plan to frequent the most.

Where the boys are

FLAMINGO

COME FISHIN

$23.00 PLUS ROD RENTAL

It was this big . . .

Stepping Out

Fort Lauderdale is in the early throes of a renaissance as the developers finally wake up to the many charms which have long made the place popular with the gay community. Namely, many pockets of architectural prettiness, the beautiful intracoastal waterways, an abundance of beach, a cosmopolitan population, and proximity to Miami. Because of its diverse population Fort Lauderdale is a place which offers multiple possibilities. Whether you're into cultural or culinary delights, lazy beach holidays, sightseeing, shopping, saunas, leather bars or dance club partying you'll find plenty to keep you distracted.

My Top Sights

Bonnet House and Gardens

The Artist's house

 Bonnet House and Gardens
900 North Birch Road, Fort Lauderdale. *See map p. 62*
 954-563-5393
www.bonnethouse.com
 10am–3pm Mon–Fri; noon–4pm Sat & Sun
 $9 house & grounds; $5 grounds only

One of a handful of shops and sights within walking distance of the beach district and the bulk of Fort Lauderdale's gay resorts and guest houses – most places have to be reached by cab or car. An historic house dating back to 1920, built by American artist Frederick Clay Bartlett, which gives a flavour of how things used to be. Paint and palette sit by an unfinished work in his studio, there's plenty of his work throughout the house, and 35 acres of estate grounds, rife with squirrel monkeys, to explore.

East Las Olas Boulevard

ℹ️ East Las Olas Boulevard, Fort Lauderdale. *See map p. 62*

Las Olas is a seemingly endless road that runs from Ocean Boulevard right through South Federal Highway, being the main route to the beach. It's way too long to navigate on foot, but if you drive or cab it to the eastern tip of Las Olas, you'll find a small upmarket strip specially designed for shopping and exploring on foot, lined with a variety of book, gift, arts and crafts and clothes shops like gay men's favourite Audace *(see p. 79)*, a range of great restaurants like Bar Amica *(see p. 85)*, popular video bar The Cathode Ray *(see p. 93)* and a chocoholic's dream, Kilwins *(see p. 81)*, to name but a few.

Jungle Queen

ℹ️ Departs Bahia Mar Yachting Center, Fort Lauderdale . *See map p. 74* 📞 954-462-5596 www.junglequeen.com
🕐 10am and 2pm daily

Touristy and over-long three-hour sightseeing cruise on an old-fashioned steamer, but it does at least give you a glimpse of the obscene wealth on show at the waterfront homes on Millionaires' Row. A live commentary points you in the direction of the home of Lee 'Six Million Dollar Man' Majors, where

Sun worshippers

Gay Beach

ℹ️ Ocean Boulevard & Sebastian Street, Fort Lauderdale. *See map p. 62*

There's a cluster of gay hotels between Bayshore Drive and Ocean Boulevard known as the Beach District, which enjoy the distinction of being a short walk from the best and most central gay beach. In a town designed for the motor car anything within walking distance is a huge bonus. Practise your tai-chi during sunrise, sunbathe with other gay girlz and boyz during the day, or have a romantic stroll at sundown. No food or alcohol allowed on the beach. Despite a heavy concentration of gay resorts, there's little else of gay interest within walking distance. Other gay beaches include locals' favourite, the quieter North East 18th Street, also John Lloyd Beach State Recreation Area, and a gay nudist beach at Haulover Beach Country Park.

Al Pacino filmed *Any Given Sunday*, and Moon River, where Henry Mancini's widow still lives. You'll encounter basking iguanas, mango and umbrella trees, boats that cost $20,000 to rent for four hours, waving residents (don't they tire of it?) and Al Capone's house. There's a brief stopover at the tiny Indian Village Zoo to see alligators, cockatoo, toucan and caged monkeys, but it's really a chance for you to waste money on trinkets. Wrap up; it can get really breezy.

Sawgrass Mills

🛈 12801 West Sunrise Boulevard, Fort Lauderdale. *See map p. 74* 📞 954-846-2350 www.sawgrassmills.com 🕐 10am–9.30pm Mon–Sat; 11am–8pm Sun

Not really a sight, as such, but somewhere you might want to spend the best part of a day. Over 300 manufacturers' outlets, brand discounters and retail stores means you can find designer goods cheaper than in the high-street stores. Labels include Converse, Perry Ellis, Benetton, Gap, J Crew, Jockey, Big 'n' Tall, Kappa, Kenneth Cole, Levi's and Guess, plus restaurants, food courts, gifts, DVDs and electronics. Shuttle service available, call 954-846-2300 for details.

South Florida Gay Charters

🛈 New River Drive (off Las Olas Boulevard), Fort Lauderdale *See map p. 74*
📞 954-768-0001 www.gaychartersflorida.com
🕐 Day, afternoon and evening cruises Thu & Sun 💲 Average price $20

Bayside day trips, tea dances and sea cruises. Shuttle service to South Beach on Saturday afternoon for shopping, dining and clubbing, returning at 2am.

Cruising queen

The wave wall

Around Town

This town can be a pain in the butt to negotiate without wheels. If you can't or won't drive cash needs to be set aside for taxi fares around town, because public transport ain't up to much. That's also why this guide will be so useful to you. A bit of forward planning will keep travel expenses to a minimum. When you venture from your resort, where possible, try to explore sights and sounds that are closest together. Explore the city piece by piece in this way. I've indicated when sights, shops and services are within walking distance. Otherwise it's safe to assume that they're not. That said, although the sheer sprawl of this town can be quite daunting, on the plus-side, that does also mean that there's an enormous diversity of things to see and do. So best get started.

Beach District and East Las Olas Boulevard

If you're wanting to spend a day in Fort Lauderdale without travelling far, forget it, this town sprawls like you wouldn't believe. However, the Beach District and East Las Olas Boulevard are at least a short 5–10-minute drive away from each other. There are places in each district that can be walked to, but don't try and march your way up Las Olas Boulevard. While it's a straight road and uncongested and therefore quick to drive, it's way longer than it appears to be on the maps and will take you forever to walk. While the gay beach is sandy and pretty, most of Ocean Boulevard is flanked by tacky restaurants.

A DAY OUT

Instead of coffee at your resort, rev up your hire car and drive up to the Floridian Restaurant (*see p. 84*) for a hearty American-style breakfast to set you up for the day. There you can eavesdrop on the muscle boys boosting their protein intake with fried breakfasts and boosting their egos gossiping

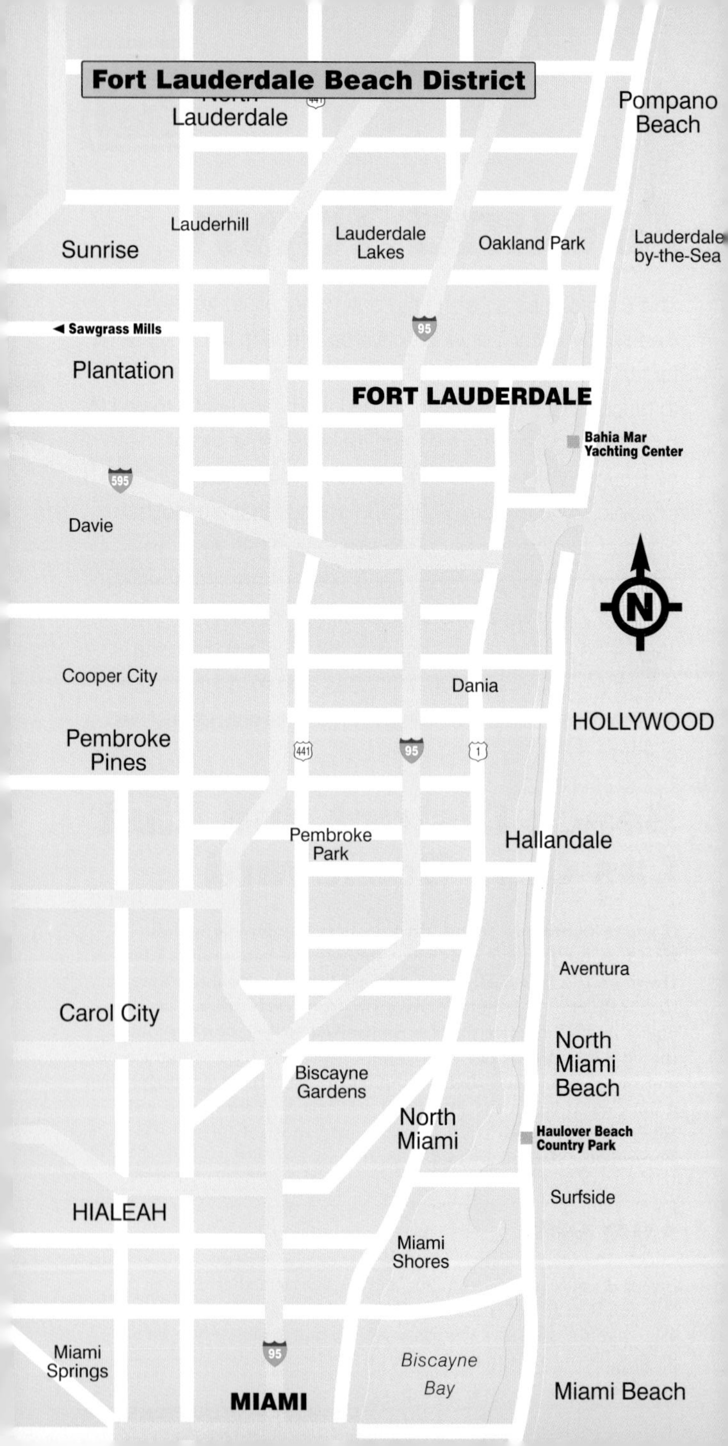

Pompano
Beach

North
Lauderdale

Sunrise

Lauderhill

Lauderdale
Lakes

Oakland Park

Lauderdale
by-the-Sea

◄ Sawgrass Mills

Plantation

FORT LAUDERDALE

Bahia Mar
Yachting Center

Davie

Cooper City

Dania

HOLLYWOOD

Pembroke
Pines

Pembroke
Park

Hallandale

Aventura

Carol City

North
Miami
Beach

Biscayne
Gardens

North
Miami

Haulover Beach
Country Park

HIALEAH

Surfside

Miami
Shores

Miami
Springs

Biscayne
Bay

MIAMI

Miami Beach

Out to Lunch

Lunch could be a snack at the nearby **Casablanca Cafe** (*see p. 83*), and a mid-afternoon beer, or a break from the sun's glare can be had a stroll away at the **Beach Place Mall** (17 Ocean Boulevard).

about the who and where of the previous night. Unusually, the Floridian doesn't accept credit cards, so make sure you take enough cash to cover your bill. Could be very embarrassing otherwise.

Walk off your breakfast with a jaunty stroll down East Las Olas Boulevard. This strip is one of the few places in Fort Lauderdale that's actually pedestrian-friendly, meaning there's a density of interesting shops within walking distance. As you browse you'll encounter all manner of local art and gift shops, bookstores, restaurants, cafés, a great confectioner's called Kilwins of Las Olas (*see p. 78*), in case you're a chocoholic, and a sexy gay store called Audace (*see p. 77*) with an exhaustive selection of designer swimwear, underwear and T-shirts, some of which you might want to model on the beach.

Now it's time for some serious shopping. Jump in the car for the short drive to upmarket mall The Galleria (*see p. 79*). Among the many Galleria stores and food courts, watch out for Saks Fifth Avenue and labels galore. A short car ride away are gay stores Clothes Encounters (*see p. 79*) and Jimmy Star (*see p. 80*), bursting with clubwear and funky, frivolous bits and pieces. Time to ditch the consumerism and stretch out for a while. So it's back in your hire car to the Gay Beach (a stretch of Ocean Boulevard just opposite Sebastian Street). It's busy and not exactly peaceful but a terrific place to people-watch and eye up the talent.

As the beach clears out, an early evening cappuccino in the coffee shop at Borders bookstore (*see p. 79*) gives you a chance to check out their extensive lesbian and gay section, and the guyz and girlz checking out the extensive lesbian and gay section. You can actually walk to Borders from the Gay Beach; it takes about 20 minutes each way. But you will need to drive back to Las Olas for dinner and a huge platter of seafood salad at Mangos (*see p. 84*). After dinner, pop across the road to the Cathode Ray (*see p. 87*) to catch the latest live quiz game or gay TV show screening. They have a hilarious dating game on Wednesdays which you should make a special effort to catch. Ready to move on? Well, none of the other bars or clubs are close to the Gay Beach or Las Olas districts, so from now on in it's time to decide which to hit. Cathode Ray stocks all the free gay listings magazines, so you can mull over the evening's options.

Catching the breeze

Wilton Manors

Wilton Drive is a long, dull and unremarkable road. But it's here and in the surrounding areas that a cluster of gay bars, clubs and businesses has sprung up. Though they might appear close on maps and guides, the sheer scale of Fort Lauderdale means that most are in fact quite a distance apart. Here again, your hire car opens up the city and makes distances that are impossible on foot seem close-by.

A DAY OUT

One day, try to get up early enough to catch the unforgettable sunrise from the Gay Beach (opposite Sebastian Street on Ocean Boulevard). It'll be all but deserted at that time except for the odd health nut practising t'ai-chi, passing joggers and the distant rumble of trucks that rake the sand early every morning. Quite a memory to take home with you.

Jump in the car and spend the day cruising around the gay shops and designer malls. There's plenty of choice, so it's really up to you to pick the places that best suit your style.

There's Wicked Leather (*see p. 81*) and Pride Stuff (*see p. 79*) for the fetishists among you.

Cruise the shops

About 12 miles west, there's designer bargains up for grabs at the massive 270-store Sawgrass Mills mall (*see p. 67*), the place for you label queens, or fetishwear and frippery at Catalog X (*see p. 77*).

All this running around will have left you flagging, so go for a spot of sunbathing. If you're tired of the Sebastian Gay Beach, take a trip out to the alternative gay beaches at North East 18th Street, John Lloyd Beach State Recreation Area ($2 entry fee) or the nude beach down at North Miami's Haulover Beach Country Park ($3.50 entry fee). Closer to home is Holiday Park – no beach but a great suntrap and popular with local gays. It's a great opportunity to eye up the talent; otherwise buy a day pass for the sun decks of The Club (*see p. 95*) or Boots (901 South West 27th Street).

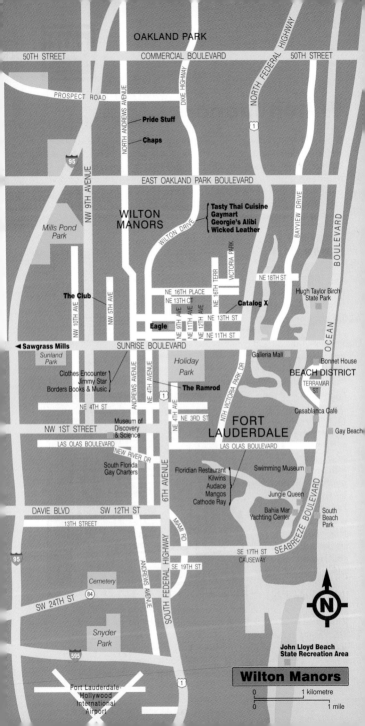

Later it's on to Tasty Thai Cuisine (*see p. 84*) for dinner. Unusual gay shopping emporium Gaymart (*see p. 80*) is part of the same block, as is popular video bar Georgie's Alibi (*see p. 89*), which makes this section of Wilton Drive one of the more popular gay hangouts. It even has its own roadside car park.

Here's looking at you

Then dash back to your resort for a change of outfit. Levis and T-shirt, leather chaps and camouflage trousers are common, but some guys just wear shorts. Now you're ready to hit The Ramrod (*see p. 90*), Eagle (*see p. 89*) or Chaps (1727 North Andrews Ext, *see p. 87*), the best three leather and Levis bars. There's no strict dress code, but you'll feel better if you look the part. Chaps has a dance floor, Ramrod is low-key and cruisey, and the Eagle is the most leathery. All have fetishwear shops either inside or next door, and all are open until the wee small hours. So, as you make your way back to your resort, you'll probably catch that south Florida sunrise again.

Pretty in pink

Shop 'til you drop

All Shopped Out

Fort Lauderdale is a funny place to shop in, just because everything is so spread out. Once reached East Las Olas is one shopping district that can be navigated on foot - for art, gifts, books and some clothing, while malls like Beach Place, The Galleria and the massive Sawgrass Mills complex are well worth a visit for famous name stores. Incidentally, near The Galleria is a cruisey Borders bookstore. And make sure you call into gay emporium Catalog X at some point for pulsating disco watches, strange sex toys and other trashy gifts and novelties.

Top of the Shops

Audace

813 East Las Olas Boulevard, Fort Lauderdale. *See map p. 74* 954-522-7503
www.audace.com 10am–10pm daily

Terrible name, great little shop. Stocking all your gay basics from skimpy underwear to T-shirts, socks, athletic swim- and sportswear from the sexiest brands like Body Body Wear, Hanro, 2(x)ist, Sauvage, Jocko, Whittall & Shon, Rips, PB pour Lui, DKNY, Hom, Gregg and Calvin Klein. Situated a few doors away from gay restaurant Bar Amica and the Cathode Ray Club.

Catalog X

850 NE 13th Street, Fort Lauderdale *See map p. 74* 954-524-5050
www.catalogx.com 10am–10pm Mon–Fri; 10am–9pm Sat; 11am–7pm Sun

This massive gay department store covering 12,000 square feet is just the place to pick up those little essentials like a vibrator that plugs into your car lighter, as well as lesbian and gay greetings cards, swim trunks, T-shirts, clubwear, erotic novelties, videos, dance CDs, DVDs, assorted porn, sex toys, condoms and lube.

Borders Books and Music

ⓘ 2240 East Sunrise Boulevard, Fort Lauderdale
See map p. 74 **ⓐ** 954-566-6335 www.borders.com
☺ 9am–11pm Mon–Sat; 9am–9pm Sun

A two-storey bookstore crammed to the drawstrings with CDs, international magazines, novels, art books, videos and DVDs. Well worth a look for their extensive lesbian & gay section and a nice in-store coffee shop overlooking the water which gets quite cruisey in the early evening. Situated just beyond The Galleria on East Sunrise Boulevard. You can walk here from the beach district if you don't mind a 25-minute trek along a main road.

The Galleria

ⓘ East Sunrise Boulevard, Fort Lauderdale
See map p. 74 **ⓐ** 954-564-1015 www.galleriamall-fl.com
☺ 10am–9pm Mon–Sat; noon–5.30pm Sun

Large upmarket mall 20 minutes from the gay resorts. Among the 150 outlets are Saks Fifth Avenue (for designer labels), Gap, Banana Republic, Speedo, Warner Bros Studio Store, Bally, Foot Locker, and a food court.

Clothes Encounters

ⓘ 1952 East Sunrise Boulevard, Fort Lauderdale *See map p. 74*
ⓐ 954-522-2228
www.clothes-encounters.com
☺ 10am–7pm Mon–Thu; 10am–10pm Fri, Sat

T-shirt emporium in the Shopping Center, with a range of adult and novelty T-shirts covering topics from superheroes and retro TV shows to sex and religion. If slogans like 'Caution. I can Go From Zero To Bitch in 2.4 seconds' make you chuckle, this place is for you.

Kilwins of Las Olas

ⓘ 809 East Las Olas Boulevard, Fort Lauderdale *See map p. 74*
ⓐ 954-523-8338 www.lasolasblvd.com/kilwins
☺ 11am–10pm Mon–Thu;
11am–midnight Fri & Sat; 1–10pm Sun

Old-fashioned confectionery, gay-friendly with flirty assistants: it must be something in the chocolate. Chocoholics will go wild for the handmade chocs, fudge, candies, ice cream, brittles, marzipan, taffy, bon bons and caramel. Unbelievably, there's even a sugar-free selection.

Chic Las Olas

Leather Master

🛈 736 NE 3rd Street, Fort Lauderdale. *NE 3rd Street: map p. 74*
📞 954-5231010
www.leathermaster.com
lmkw@bellsouth.net
🕗 11am–9pm Tues–Sat; noon–6pm Sun; Closed Mon

Sister (or should that be brother) store to the Key West staple, stocking porno DVDs, sex toys and accessories, condoms, lube and leatherwear.

Swap Shop

🛈 3291 West Sunrise Boulevard, Fort Lauderdale. *Sunrise Boulevard: map p. 62* 📞 954-791-7927
🕗 11am–10pm daily
🎟 Free admission

The largest outdoor/indoor flea market and drive-in cinema in the US. A massive 150,000 square foot of trashy goods to sift through: clothes, electrical goods, martial arts weapons, food, and always the odd bargain. The costumed dancing dogs and musical fountains take the world of showbiz to an all-time low.

Gay department store

Pride Stuff

🛈 1735 North Andrews Avenue, Fort Lauderdale *Andrews Avenue: map p. 74* 📞 954-764-0394
www.pridestuff.com 🕗 noon–midnight daily

Next door to Chaps leather club. Dance CDs, porn videos, fetishwear and accessories, cards and calendars, adult toys, stickers, leather, lubes, videos and poppers. If you've a fuller figure, check out their bear wear.

For glamour girls

Shop Around

Looks tasty

BEACH PLACE

ℹ️ 17 Ocean Boulevard, Fort Lauderdale

📠 954-760-9570

🕐 11am–10pm Mon–Thu; 11am–midnight Fri and Sat

Three floors of shopping and dining just up from the Gay Beach. You might want to cool off with a drink here, enjoy a Guinness at the Irish Pub, pick up some basics from Sunglass Hut, Speedo and Gap, or set yourself up with a healthy snack at the General Nutrition Center.

GAYMART

ℹ️ 2240 Wilton Drive, Wilton Manors, Fort Lauderdale

📠 954-630-0360

🕐 10am–10pm Mon– Thu & Sun; 10am–midnight Fri and Sat

Gay trash emporium with clothes, gifts and novelties. Take a look, it's just across the car park from Tasty Thai and Georgie's Alibi.

IN THE PINK BOOKS

ℹ️ 2205 Wilton Drive, Wilton Manors, Fort Lauderdale

📠 954-566-0166 email: inthepinkbook s@yahoo.com

🕐 noon–7pm Wed–Sat; noon–5pm Sun

Gay and lesbian bookstore stocking a limited range of novels, magazines, novelties and cards. Watch out for flyers giving you a 10% discount on books.

JIMMY STAR

ℹ️ 1940 East Sunrise Boulevard, Fort Lauderdale

📠 954-768-0043 www.jimmystar.com

🕐 11am–7pm Mon–Thu; 11am–10pm Fri and Sat; 11am–5pm Sun

Funky discount designer store with all the loud, sparkly disco fashions you could want, plus shoes and fetish gear.

PRIDE FACTORY

ℹ️ 845 North Federal Highway, Fort Lauderdale

📠 954-463-6600

🕐 noon–8pm daily

Situated right by locals' bar The Cubby Hole, Pride Factory is a gay superstore carrying a little of everything including an extensive selection of dirty videos, some books, loads of magazines, T-shirts and some rather tasteless clubwear, fetish wear and accessories, but prominently heaps of trashy, novelty stuff.

ZOO 14

ℹ️ 918 North Federal Highway, Fort Lauderdale

📞 945-462-7373

🕐 10am–8pm Mon–Sat; noon–5pm Sun

Trashy and raunchy gay menswear. If loud shirts, lycra

Lycra heaven

T-shirts and leopard-skin undies are your thing, then you'll be in heaven here.

LEATHER WERKS

ℹ️ 1226 NE 4th Avenue, Fort Lauderdale

📞 954-761-1236

email: info@Leather Werks.com

🕐 noon–8pm Mon–Sat; 1–6pm Sun

Slip into something a little less comfortable with custom-made leatherwear, hats, body jewellery, harnesses, hoods, piercing, chaps and restraints.

WICKED LEATHER

ℹ️ 2422 Wilton Drive, Wilton Manors, Fort Lauderdale

📞 954-564-7529

www.wickedleather.com

🕐 11am–9pm Tues–Sat; 1–6pm Sun

Sex toys, accessories and porn, including rare XXX videos from cult director Dick Wadd.

Naughty store

Dine inside or out

Eating Out

While overall the eating here may not quite be of the exceptional standards enjoyed on Miami Beach, there's still plenty of choice, portions are big and prices pitched slightly lower. With drive-in fast food joints almost on every corner, it seemed harder to resist an instant fix from junk food here. . .

Cream of the Cuisine

Bar Amica

1301 Las Olas Boulevard, Fort Lauderdale. *Las Olas Boulevard: map p. 74* 954-467-3266 11.30am–11pm Sun–Thu; 11.30am– 11.30pm Fri and Sat

The following price guides have been used for eating out and indicate the price for a main course:

= cheap = under $10

= moderate = $10–$20

= expensive = over $20

Large, sophisticated gay bistro. American cuisine with an Italian spin. Great food, big portions, live blues and jazz some evenings and afternoons, a few outdoor tables, and it's close to the Cathode Ray Bar. Highly recommended.

Brasserie Las Olas

333 East Las Olas Boulevard. *Las Olas Boulevard: map p. 74* 954-779-7374 11am–11pm Mon–Fri; 9am–5pm Sat and Sun

Upmarket brasserie and bar serving good-quality American staples among sumptuous grand plantation-style decor. Salads, steaks, grills, homemade burgers, oven-baked pizza, soups and salads. Jazz at weekends.

Casablanca Cafe

3049 Alhambra Street. *See map p. 74* 954-764-3500 11am–11pm daily

Gay-friendly cheap eats near the gay beach. Indoor and covered outdoor tables afford a view of the Ocean Boulevard and the Atlantic, with live jazz most evenings.

Yummy pancakes

Floridian Restaurant

ⓘ 1410 East Las Olas Boulevard. *See map p. 74*

📷 954-463-4041

🕐 24 hours daily

Good for late-night snacks and popular for big American breakfasts – grilled sandwiches, pancakes, steak and eggs, and posh burgers. Lo-cal platters too.

Henry's China House

ⓘ 745 SE 17th Street Causeway   **🕐** 11am–10.30pm Mon–Sat

Fort Lauderdale's first Chinese restaurant (opened in 1959) and still one of the best. Healthy Szechuan, Mandarin and Cantonese cuisine.

Mangos

ⓘ 904 East Las Olas Boulevard, Fort Lauderdale *See map p. 74*   **📷** 954-523-5001   **🕐** 11am–2am Mon–Thu and Sun; 11am–1am Fri and Sat

One of my favourites. Indoor or sidewalk dining in the heart of the Las Olas, and close to Audace, Bar Amica and the Cathode Ray video bar. Burgers, salads, grilled chicken and pasta dishes. We returned time and again for their unbeatable seafood salad. Live music most evenings.

Quarterdeck

ⓘ 2933 Las Olas Boulevar. Las Olas Boulevard: map p. 74   **📷** 954-525-2010

🕐 11am–2am Mon Mon–Thu;11am–3am Fri and Sat

Low-key seafood bar and grill, a short walk from the Gay Beach. Reasonably priced standards and snow crab legs, coconut shrimp, dolphin Caesar salad. Dine inside, or out, on novel swing seats.

Tasty Thai Cuisine

ⓘ 2254 Wilton Drive, Wilton Manors *See map p. 74*   **📷** 954-396-3177   **🕐** 11am–3pm Mon–Fri; 5–11pm Sun and Mon

Excellent Pad Thai, jumbo shrimp, Thai salads and other spicy delicacies served by flirtatious young Asian waiters. A favourite with the locals.

CHARDEES

 2209 Wilton Drive (NE 4th Avenue), Wilton Manors

954-563-1800

4.30pm daily cocktails; 6–10pm Sun–Thu; 6–11pm Fri and Sat

Fast food outlet

Fill up on simple American cuisine from omelette to ribs served by snappily dressed waiters, all to the strains of karaoke, cabaret or tinkering piano at this buffet restaurant and cocktail lounge. Long-running gay haunt, popular with the 50+ grey gay crowd and often referred to as 'God's waiting room'. Oh, the cheek of it!

LE Q BISTRO & LOUNGE

 2761 East Oakland Park Boulevard

954-563-5544

www.hometown.aol.com/le Qfrenchbistro

5pm–1am Tues–Sun; Closed Mon

Laid-back gay restaurant and piano bar serving fine French cuisine, sometimes with live singers, cabaret or musicians. Special offers for diners between 5pm and 6pm on Tuesday,

Wednesday and Sunday. All in all, attracts a fashionable, smart-casual 20s and 30s crowd. It's recommended that you reserve your table.

SAWDEE THAI RESTAURANT

 2364 North Federal Highway, Union Planters Bank Plaza

954-537-9391

5–10pm Mon–Fri and Sun; 3.30–10pm Sat

Cheap and cheerful spicy bites, ranging from the usual noodle, fried rice and curry dishes to vegetarian and tofu choices and delicacies like soft shell crab and frogs' legs. Live music every third Friday and Saturday of the month. Gay-friendly.

Whats for lunch?

Best of the Rest

Don't miss the bus

Out on the Town

As with everything in Fort Lauderdale, work the town area by area when you can to keep your cab fares down. One night out might be cruising a cluster of leather bars. Another might be taking in a mixture of shops, restaurants and bars on East Las Olas or Wilton Manors, or maybe you'll divide the night between nearby dance clubs like The Sea Monster and The Copa. The diverse nightlife is a major highlight of the town.

My Top Clubs

Cathode Ray Club

1307 East Las Olas Boulevard, Fort Lauderdale. *See map p. 74* 954-462-8611 www.cathoderayusa.com 2pm–2am Mon–Sun; 2pm–3am Fri and Sat Free

One of my favourites. Busy video bar with games room, bar snacks, screenings of popular camp TV shows like *Queer As Folk* and *The Weakest Link*, and occasional live entertainment. Check out Wednesday's popular stage show 'The Dating Gayme' which is broadcast live round the world on the internet on www.DatingGayme.com. As ever in Fort Lauderdale, dress casual; 20s–40s crowd.

Chaps

1727 North Andrews Way, Fort Lauderdale. *See map p. 74* 954-767-0027 2pm–2am Mon–Thu and Sun; 2pm–3am Fri and Sat Free

A Levis and leather club with a large dance floor. The sight of seeing seriously butch mustachioed leathermen dancing to Kylie is something to behold, but this place is lots of fun. Lots of dark nooks and crannies. One popular room just behind the bar has no lighting at all! Dance floor, back room and Pride Stuff gay shop next door. Casual, leather or Levis; crowd ranges from 30s–50s.

Coliseum

ℹ️ 2520 South Miami Road, Fort Lauderdale

📞 954-832-0100

www.coliseumnightclub.com

🕐 10pm–6am Fri and Sat

💲 Free

Dance yourself dizzy

Fort Lauderdale's largest dance club is a huge former cinema complex. There's a quieter bar room with seating, three bars, a huge dance floor and a gallery level to spy the talent from. We went for their packed Saturday night happy house danceathon and had an absolute blast. Highly recommended. Dress casual; 20s and 30s crowd.

Copa

ℹ️ 2800 South Federal Highway, Fort Lauderdale. Federal Highway: map p. 74

📞 954-463-1507

www.copaboy.com

🕐 10pm–late daily

💲 Free

Perennial L-shaped dance club which gets very busy on Friday and Saturday nights. A long-reigning staple of the scene, Copa attracts quite a mix of people and age groups. There's a never-ending parade of new nights and gimmicks during the week, so call ahead for the latest prices and line-ups. Just down the road from Inn Leather. Diverse 20s–40s crowd; dress casual.

Cubby Hole

ℹ️ 823 North Federal Highway, Fort Lauderdale. Federal Highway: map p. 74

📞 954-728-9001 🕐 11am–2am Mon–Sat; noon–2am Sun 💲 Free

Friendly locals' bar on the same block as gay store The Pride Factory. Pool table, porn screens, a collection of kitsch modern lamps and helpfully a bank of computers giving free internet access to customers. Friendly, mainly local 20s–50s crowd; dress casual.

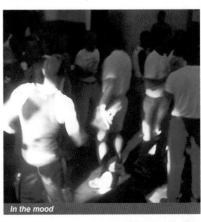
In the mood

Eagle

ⓘ 1951 NW 9th Avenue, Fort
Lauderdale. *See map p. 74*
⊘ 954-462-7224 www.eaglebar.net
⊘ 3pm–3am Fri and Sat; 3pm–2am
Sun–Thu **⊘** Free

The furthest to reach of all the
leather bars, but one of the
largest and raunchiest ones.
Dark and industrial-looking
with a labyrinth of bar rooms
and dark corners to explore, plus
an on-site sex shop stocking
everything from Daddy's cigars
to poppers, condoms and
fetishwear and accessories. Dress
up in leather, Levis or fetishwear
to fit in with the cruisey crowd
ranging from 20s–50s.

Georgie's Alibi

ⓘ 2266 Wilton Drive (NE 4th Avenue),
Wilton Manors, Fort Lauderdale. *See
map p. 74*
⊘ 954-565-2526
www.georgiesalibi.com
⊘ 11am–2am Mon–Fri; 11am–3am
Sat; noon–2am Sun **⊘** Free

Popular gay cocktail bar showing
all the latest pop video promos,
with regular cabaret and drinks
promotions. Georgie's is always
busy with a completely diverse
crowd. There's also an outdoor
dining area serving snack food
if you're feeling peckish. Dress
smart or casual to blend in with
the diverse 20s–40s crowd of
young bucks and after-work
drinkers.

Las Olas after dark

Ramrod

ⓘ 1508 NE 4th Avenue, Fort Lauderdale.
See map p. 62 🔗 954-763-8219
www.ramrodbar.com 🕐 3pm–3am Fri
and Sat; 3pm–2am Sun–Thu 🎟 Free

Our favourite leather, Levis and
uniform bar playing a compulsive
mix of European retro, dance and
rock music. You'll find indoor and
outdoor bars, theme nights and
back rooms galore. Browse there,
or in the friendly Dungeon Bear
Leather Inc fetishwear shop by the
club entrance. You might want to
head here for Thursday's popular
Battle Of The Bulge contest, when
contestants strip to their undies to
see who has the biggest packet.
Dress casual, leather or Levis; 30s–
50s crowd.

Sea Monster

ⓘ 2 South New River Drive, Fort
Lauderdale 🔗 954-463-4641
🕐 10pm–2am Thu–Mon; 9pm–3am Fri
and Sat; 4pm–2am Sun 🎟 Free
Sunday, otherwise prices vary

Huge, gay-owned and run dance
club right on the water. Sunday's
T-Dance is an absolute must with
a smattering of drag queens and
young gay party people, dressed
down of course, or showing off
those pumped-up pecs. Sunday
starts off with light disco vibes
(4–8pm) then gets a little more
tough with hard house and
HiNRG (8pm–closing). Check
local press for a rundown of ever-
changing nights. Dress clubwear or
casual; crowd 20s–40s.

Leather and Levis

Hanky panky?

All Clubbed Out

BILL'S FILLING STATION

ℹ️ NE 11th & NE 13th Street, Fort Lauderdale

📞 954-525-9403

🕐 11am–2am Mon–Thu; 11am–3am Fri and Sat; noon–2am Sun

💲 Free

Locals' gay bar with two pool tables, central oval-shaped bar and outside patio bar. Inside, the walls are strung with gay motor memorabilia including licence plates. I spotted one with the registration GAY69. Mainly men, but there's a particularly lesbian-friendly Friday nighter. Local crowd 30s–50s; dress casual.

BOOTS

ℹ️ 901 SW 27th Avenue, Fort Lauderdale

📞 954-792-9177

🕐 noon–3am Fri and Sat; noon–2am Sun–Thu

💲 Free

Leathers, Levis, rubber and fetishwear are the things to wear here in the evenings, but if you pop in to sun-bathe during the day, you can go nude on their open-air sun-deck. Watch out for their famous flea market sales. Dress casual or in leather, Levis or fetishwear for a laid-back 30s–50s crowd.

JOHNNY'S

ℹ️ 1116 West Broward Boulevard, Fort Lauderdale

📞 954-522-5931

www.johnnysboys.com

🕐 10am–2am Mon–Sat; 10am–3am Fri and Sat; noon–2am Sun 💲 Free

Male revue bar,

These boots were made for walking

complete with young
go-go boys strutting
their stuff. Regular
pool tournaments,
bar snacks available,
as well as compli-
mentary buffets and
wet jock contests.
Dress casual for this
friendly local crowd
who are mainly in
their 30s and 40s.

SAINT

📍 1000 State Road 84,
Fort Lauderdale

📞 954-525-7883
www.thesaintnightclub.net
🕐 7 nights

Three-room dance
and go-go boy bar
with hot young bucks
gyrating in a quite
sluttish fashion.
Lesbians hold court
here most Saturday
nights, otherwise guyz
rule the roost with a
weekly line-up of
Shower Shows,
weekly Thursday night
Southern Country

line-dancing (Yee-ha!),
Friday night special
events and alter ego
fetish theme nights on
the second Saturday of
the month. With so
many choices on offer,
club nights go in and
out of fashion quickly
in Fort Lauderdale and
can change music
policy or close with
little warning, so call
ahead or check the
local gay press for
their latest programme
of events.

Festivals and Annual Parties

Time to party

STONEWALL STREET FESTIVAL & PARADE
LATE JUNE

📞 954-745-7070
www.pgfl.org

Annual lesbian and
gay pride free
festival on Wilton
Manors Drive, with
an official Stonewall
party at one of the
local nightspots
that evening.

DUNGEON 601
OCTOBER

📍 Leather University, PO Box 39372, Fort Lauderdale FL 33339

📞 954-761-9828 email: registrar@leatheru.com www.LeatherU.com

💲 $150–$200

Annual weekend of hands-on workshops, demos, seminars and
leather play, planned by and produced for gay men and lesbians.

Working Out

OUTLINES

THE CLUB
110 NW 5th Avenue
954-525-3344
www.the-clubs.com
24 hours daily
Day passes $18; Day pass with private room $28

Very popular gay sauna with an ultra-modern stylish decor, tasteful furnishings and so many facilities it's known locally as the Country Club. A youngish crowd from both Fort Lauderdale and Miami take advantage of the dry sauna, steam room, gym with free weights and treadmills, private dressing rooms, multi-level sundeck, outside whirlpool, shower room and swimming pool. 20s and 30s.

CLUBHOUSE II
2650 East Oakland Park Boulevard
954-566-6750
24 hours daily
Membership $8 (with photo ID); 8am–4pm $9; otherwise $14; Private rooms $20–$26

Tuesday is Leather Night at this busy gay sauna, and it's those masculine leather and Levis types you can expect to find frolicking here all week long in the whirlpool. Facilities include video room, dry sauna, steam room, showers, juice bar, gym and private suites. 30s–50s crowd.

GOLD COAST ROLLER RINK
2604 South Federal Highway
954-523-6783
8pm–midnight Tues
$4 with your own skates; $5 to hire skates; $6 to hire rollerblades

The US's oldest gay rollerskating session. A kind of cruise as you bruise! Wildfire private skate parties where clothing is optional. Nude skating every three months.

HOLIDAY PARK
South of Sunrise Boulevard & NE 12th Avenue

A great place for a jog if you're fit enough, or perhaps just a bracing stroll day or night. The car park might be of interest.

WELLNESS CENTER
Gay & Lesbian Community Center, 1717 North Andrews Avenue
9am–10pm Mon–Fri; 9am–5pm Sat and Sun
Free

Drop-in advice and health centre and café for gay men and lesbians. A range of suncreams and after-sun skin treatments with vitamin E and aloe vera.

WILD OATS COMMUNITY MARKET
2501 East Sunrise Boulevard
954-566-9333
8am–10pm daily

Heath food super-market where you can pick up natural groceries, organic produce, vitamins and supplements and bodycare products. Great salad bar, *sushi,* and aloe vera skin products.

Checking In

Most of Fort Lauderdale's best gay resorts centre on an scenic area known as the Beach District. Here you're beside the ocean near one of the gay beaches opposite Sebastian Street, and within walking distance of The Galleria and Beach Place malls, but far from most good restaurants and the bar and club scene. If driving or cabs are going to be a particular issue, then you might choose to stay closer to the eateries and nightlife of Wilton Manors (Cabanas Guesthouse) or East Las Olas (Pineapple Point). Don't be too hasty, and weigh up all the pros and cons - you might be missing out on some great accommodations...

The Best Beds

Blue Dolphin

ⓘ 725 N. Birch Road
☏ 954-565-8437
www.bluedolphinhotel.com
Fax: 954-565-6015
▮ ②

The following price guides have been used for accommodation, per room per night :

① = cheap = under $75
② = moderate = $75 – $200
③ = expensive = $200 and over

One of the best hotels catering for the Levis and leather brigade. Blue Dolphin is a secluded gay-owned hotel, run by a friendly British gay couple. Behind the striking turquoise and lilac exterior lie 18 themed rooms, including Western style – with cowboy erotica and Indian headdress – and Master Bedroom, with leather chairs and a teddy bear in a sling. Clothing is optional beside the heated courtyard pool, there's a barbecue area, and the owners are fluent in German.

Coral Reef Guest House

ℹ 2609 NE 13th Court.
NE 13th Court: *map p. 74*
✆ 954-568-0292
email: Coralref@aol.com
www.coralreefguest-house.com
Fax: 954- 568-1992

⊟ ② – ③

This charming, secluded and central, clothing-optional, friendly guest house comes highly

Friendly guest house

recommended. All but one of the individually designed rooms and studios overlook the pool and Jacuzzi. All have private baths, cable TV/video and phone, some even have private patios. Located in a quiet residential area of Middle River. The Galleria and Borders are near, the Gay Beach is a 20-minute walk away, and the Wilton Manors a short drive. Coral Reef used to be a leather resort, so watch out for the odd giveaway. No smoking indoors.

Flamingo Resort

ℹ 2727 Terramar Street. *Terramar Street: map p. 74*
✆ 954-561-4658 email: info@flamingo resort.com
www.flamingoresort.com Fax: 954-566-2688. **⊟ ②** (16 Dec–15 Apr);
① – ② (16 Apr–15 Dec)

Very sociable art-deco resort. All rooms overlook a large, central,

palmed courtyard sundeck, where a lot of the guests pass the day chatting and basking in the tropical sunshine, and kitsch pink neon flamingos and coloured lights add some night-time magic. There's cable TV, telephone and air-conditioning in every room. Plus free internet, and use of several bicycles – which is a big plus in such a vast town – with a workout room to keep you buff. Laundry facilities. Men only. Clothing optional.

Anyone for water polo?

The Grand

ℹ 539 North Birch Road. *Birch Road: map p. 74* **📞** 954-630-3000
email: info@grandresort.net
www.grandresort.net
Fax: 954-630-3003

Newly remodelled luxurious gay accommodation near the Sebastian Street Gay Beach, with a smart, tastefully modern decor. Rooftop solarium, oversized pool, outdoor Jacuzzi, fitness centre, café and high sundeck that affords a view of the Atlantic ocean a few blocks away. Free internet access, magazines and newspapers daily.
Plus there's a scuba diving package available with a gay instructor. The friendly staff are multilingual. Friendly and stylish, The Grand is definitely the place to stop over for sophisticated international travellers who are tired of impersonal business hotels.

Pineapple Point

ℹ 315 NE 16th Terrace, Victoria Park. *NE16th Terrace: map p. 74*
📞 954-527-0094
email: info@pineapplepoint.com
www.pineapplepoint.com
Fax: 954-527-0705

In a city designed for the car, Pineapple Point is one of the few resorts near any gay bars or decent restaurants. Being within walking distance of East Las Olas Boulevard means you have Audace, the Cathode Ray Club, Mangos and Bar Amica restaurants on your doorstep, which could help keep cab costs down if you don't drive. It's also newly renovated and very luxurious here, with landscaped gardens, pool and ten-man Jacuzzi. Free board games, magazines and newspapers in the lounge. Rooms have nice touches like goose-feather pillows, cable TV, VCR, fridges and private bathrooms; a few have their own sundeck. No smoking in the rooms. Like Royal Palms, only more sedate.

Royal Palms

ℹ 2901 Terramar Street. *Terramar Street: map p. 74* **📞** 954-564-6444 email: royalpalms@aol.com www.royalpalms.com Fax: 954-564-6443

Sumptuous tropical surroundings, totally immaculate rooms and a meticulous attention to detail characterise this long-standing, award-winning gay resort. Free breakfast, snacks, drinks and beers throughout the day. There's a free library of CDs, and movies. Rooms feature bathrooms, cable TV, video and CD player. The most luxurious suites have a separate lounge room with its own TV/video and CD player, and verandas offering views of the grounds. Outside is a large sundeck, hammock, cocktail bar and Jacuzzi beside a large swimming pool fed by a waterfall. Relaxed and friendly ambience, despite the luxury. Almost entirely men, but women welcome. Clothing optional.

Frolicking at the Royal Palms

Saint Sebastian Guest House

🛈 2835 Terramar Street. *Terramar Street: map p. 74* 📠 954-568-6161
www.saintsebastianhotel.com Fax: 954-568-8209 📖 ① – ②

Flawless colonial-style villa resort just three blocks from the Gay Beach at Saint Sebastian Street. New heated plunge pool, fountains, wicker furnishings, cacti, palms and tropical vegetation as far as the eye can see. The good-sized rooms have private baths, cable TV, video, telephone and fridge. There's a communal lounge/computer room, library and a shower for late checkers.

Flying the flag at the Saint Sebastian

Venice Beach Guest Quarters

I 552 North Birch Road. *North Birch Road: map p. 74* I 954-564-9601 email: veniceqtrs@aol.com www.veniceqtrs.com Fax: 954-564-5618 I

Beautiful, modern and well-maintained, Venice Beach Guest Quarters is a gay-run resort attracting a mixed gay/straight clientele. Clothing optional on the secluded wooden rooftop sundeck. Whirlpool, gym, coin-operated laundry, free internet and video library. Gay-owned and run, but attracting a mixed gay/straight clientele.
Rooms have video, CD and phone, while a few have private patios. Outside, the well-stocked garden courtyard is crawling with lanterns, wicker garden furniture, wrought-iron geckos, and a few real ones. No smoking indoors.

Villa Venice

2900 Terramar Street. *Terramar Street: map p. 74*
954-564-7855 email: villaven@bellsouth.net www.villavenice.com Fax: 954-564-7866

Bright, characterful courtyard-style hotel with 14 rooms all featuring private bath, cable TV, fridge and coffee makers. Some with full kitchens. Built on three tiered levels, the rooms are light and airy with ceiling-to-floor windows giving views over the grounds and quiet street beyond. There's a lift and a large, 8ft-deep pool. Caters for men and women. Clothing optional.

The Worthington

I 543 North Birch Road. *North Birch Road: map p. 74* 954-563-6819 www.worthguesthouse I

Immaculate, recently decorated all-male resort close to the Sebastian Street Gay Beach.
A well-planted tropical garden and brick deck is studded with a large, 7ft-deep pool.
Rooms are clean and modern with cable TV, video, CD player, fridge, phone (with data port) and queen- or king-sized beds. Some rooms have full kitchens and there are laundry facilities, but as clothing is optional you might not dirty much. Surprisingly good value.

The tropical garden at the Orton Terrace

Sleeping Around

INN LEATHER

ⓘ 610 SE 19th Street

✆ 954-467-1444

www.innleather.com

Fax: 954-467-1444

 ① – **②**

Newly opened no-frills leather resort. Clean but basic. Maid service is only on request and may be charged for. All rooms have phones, but the line is communal and only makes local calls. However, if you insist on a leather sling in every room this could be for you. All rooms with cable TV and bathroom. Large pool, barbecue area, outdoor sling beside the hot tub. Inn Leather hosts wild Saturday-night parties staged by outside organisers. Day passes available.

BEACH DISTRICT

BRIGANTINE

ⓘ 2831 Vistamar Street

✆ 954-565-6911

email: info@brigantine hotel.com

www.brigantinehotel.com

Fax: 954-565-8911

 ②

Good-quality budget accommodation near the Gay Beach. Cable TV/VCR, phone, microwave, refrigerator and coffee maker in all rooms.

ORTON TERRACE

ⓘ 606 Orton Avenue

✆ 954-566-5068

email: orton@orton terrace.com

www.ortonterrace.com

Fax: 954-564-8646

 ① – **③**

Pleasant, 13-room, moderately-priced motel in a shady tropical garden, with a large heated pool and a choice of one and two bedroom suites, some with their own sundeck. Near the Gay Beach, The Galleria and Borders. Free internet access in communal lounge. Men only.

VICTORIA PARK

MANGROVE VILLAS

ⓘ 1100 North Victoria Park Road

✆ 954-527-5250 email: villasftl@aol.com

www.mangrovevillas.com

②

Clean, comfortable, clothing optional resort for guys. Large pool and sundeck, TV/video and queen-sized beds. Studios, villas and extended-stay apartments. Near to cruisey Holiday Park and The Galleria, and with the gay scene at Wilton Manors little more than a short drive away you're close to the fun.

WILTON MANORS

CABANAS GUEST HOUSE
 2209 NE 26th Street
954-564-7764
email: info@thecabanas guesthouse.com

www.thecabanasguest house.com

Fabulous resort nestled on the banks of Middle River, and just on the edge of Wilton Manors where lots of gay bars, leather clubs and shops are situated. If you're relying on cabs to get you around, a resort in Wilton Manors or Victoria Park will at least keep the cab journeys short. However, getting to the good dance clubs can be quite a drive.

SEA GRAPE HOUSE
 1109 NE 16th Place
954-525-6586
email: CGrapeHse@aol.com
www.seagrape.com
Fax: 954-525-0586

Secluded B & B inn, which, at four blocks away, is closest to the Wilton Manors scene. Rooms have double beds, TV and VCR, large pool, sundeck, tropical gardens, and video library. Mostly men. Free continental breakfast and cocktails. Clothing is optional at the pool.

Contemplating a dip

Top up that tan

Key West

One of the bars near Mallory Square has a plaque saying: 'There is more to life than increasing its speed – *Gandhi*.' This pretty much sums up the local attitude – the pace of life here is casual and very sedate. Key West is a smallish town that can be navigated on foot. It doesn't really live up to its reputation as one of the more famous gay hotspots, because there isn't that much gay life beyond the resorts and guest houses. Gay residents complain that an increase in cruise liners docking in Key West has brought too many straights to town and driven much of the gay population away, and there certainly is a feeling that things aren't as gay as they used to be. Nonetheless, Key West is tranquil, beautiful and gay-friendly. There is a (windswept) gay beach at the appropriately named Dick Dock on Reynolds Street, but most people go to the pool at their guest house. The cluster of gay bars and clubs sit among their straight counterparts on and around Duval Street, but I found the atmosphere completely non-threatening. Don't expect dance clubs; the scene is mainly of the video, drag show and go-go boy bar variety, with a token leather club and an open-air Sunday tea-dance.

Forget raving, get into step with the lackadaisical local pace: turn on, tune in and chill out.

Key West – sunlight shining on white buildings

ERNEST HEMINGWAY
HOME
OPEN 9.00 A.M. 5.00 PM ADMISSION
ADULTS $9.00 CHILD $5.00

For whom the bell tolls?

Stepping Out

See the island as the first Spanish settlers did, as a mirage-like smudge on the horizon while you race through the Atlantic surf on one of the many gay Charter cruises. However, back on dry land the island is small enough to be explored by foot or bicycle which you can hire for the day.

My Top Sights

Brigadoon

Next stop Cuba

🛈 201 William Street, Old Town Key West, Dock E, Bight Marina. *See map p. 112*

📞 305-923-7245
www.captainstevekw.com

🕐 11am daily

💲 Snorkel cruise $70 (includes lunch, beer and soft drink); Sunset sails $35 (includes beer and wine)

Captain Steve takes up to six guys on a leisurely five-hour gay cruise along the coral reef. Snorkelling equipment and instruction are provided. The tan you'll have to work on yourself, but it could be all-over as swimsuits are optional!

Clione Butterfly of the Sea

🛈 Participants are collected from their hotels

📞 305-292-2231/305-296-1433/305-304-7434 ww.schoonerclione.com

🕐 noon–sunset winter, 2pm–sunset summer

💲 $70 per person in the winter; $70 per person in the summer

Sailing, reef snorkelling, swimming and nude sunbathing provided by the largest gay-owned and run sail charters in Key West. Do take some strong sunblock for those extra sensitive bits.

Ernest Hemingway Home & Museum

Home of six-toed cats

ⓘ 907 Whitehead Street, Key West.
See map p. 112
☎ 305-294-1136
www.hemingwayhome.com
🕐 9am–5pm daily
💲 $6.50

See Marilyn Monroe reclining on the bed, Zsa Zsa Gabor, Ida Lupino and Pablo Picasso sunbathing in the garden, and Frank Sinatra nibbling his bottom. Not the actual celebrities, of course, but the famously deformed Hemingway cats, many of which boast extra toes.

Once home to the late Nobel Prize-winning author Ernest Hemingway, who penned *For Whom the Bell Tolls* and *To Have and Have Not*, this picturesque 1930s house and walking tour is a testament to the eccentric novelist.

Ghost Tours of Key West

ⓘ Departs from Holiday Inn La Concha Hotel, 430 Duval Street, Key West. *See map p. 112*
☎ 305-294-9255
www.hauntedtours.com
💲 Nightly tours $18; Reservations required

Typical Key West historic architecture

A leisurely hour-and-a-half walking tour of Key West Old Town that might just put the willies up you. Hear local legends about murder, pirate treasure, wreckers, yellow fever, strange apparitions and yarns about possessed dollies and corpse-marrying sickos. You'd think they'd prefer to keep a lid on this sort of gossip.

Performing on the street

Sunset Celebration

ℹ️ Mallory Square, 1 Whitehead Street, Key West. *See map p. 112*

📞 305-296-4557

🕐 About an hour before sunset daily

Key West's famous sunset celebration may have hippy origins, but now it's commercial and touristy. Street performers, tightrope walkers, local drunks, fire-eaters, and sword swallowers compete for your attention and pass the hat when they have it. Still compulsive viewing, but take plenty of dollar bills.

Time Out Charters

ℹ️ Garrison Bight Marina, Key West. *See map p. 112* 📞 305-304-2128 www.gaytraveling.com/timeout 🕐 10am and 1pm (4pm summer) 🤿 Snorkel cruise $50 per person; Sunset cruise $175 per boat

Sexy sea dog Captain Tom provides daily boat cruises, weather and conditions permitting, especially tailored for gay men. Cap'n Tom can also show you the ropes – or barnacles, rather – with snorkelling instruction for the uninitiated.

Take a cruise

You're never far from the nautical on Key West

out AROUND

Around Town

Key West

Key West contrasts the relative bustle of Duval Street with the sleepy small-town feel around the guest houses just a few blocks away. Great tracts of ocean and sky, palms and blooms fill your vision, while old buildings, evocative street names and other reminders of the town's conspicuous 19th-century wealth from smuggling, wrecking and piracy, crop up unexpectedly wherever you turn. In Key West the sun almost always shines, and as it is situated at the southernmost tip of America you'll feel quite removed from the rest of the US country. In fact, you're actually much closer to Cuba.

A DAY OUT

Try breakfast at Camille's (*see p. 119*) to kick-start the day with a sugar high from French toast dripping with chocolate sauce, vast waffles doused in mango, passion fruit and coconut, or breakfast eggs sunny side up. This is a good starting point as Duval Street is also the main drag for shopping. Don't miss Graffiti (*see p. 115*) for some gay basics like tight T-shirts, swimwear and underwear.

Something vaguely cerebral might be an antidote, so check out Ernest Hemingway's Home and Museum (*see p. 108*). The free guided tour is worth taking to catch up on this eccentric novelist and philanderer. If you like those mustachioed daddy types you might think he was quite cute too. Straight though. Or else head for the pool (the beach is windy and rough underfoot), not forgetting to stop off at Flaming Maggie's (*see p. 115*) to pick up a good book.

When you've tired of solitude, head for the chaos and touristy trinkets of Mallory Square (near Front Street). An hour before sunset is the Sunset Celebration with jugglers, fire-eaters and other street performers. Too crowded for comfort? Then as night falls enrol on one of the Ghost Tours of Key West (*see p. 108*), where you'll learn about wreckers, cut-throat pirates, and a nasty-sounding terminal outbreak of yellow fever. Afterwards you'll want to swap ghost stories over dinner. Head for Denny's Diner (*see p. 120*) for tasty cheap eats in a strangely 50s setting, or for somewhere more intimate and upscale Cafe Sole (*see p. 119*). After dinner, it's time to take Duval Street by storm. Virtually all the gay bars and clubs are located here, most have entertainment in the form of bouncy pop promo videos, groin-thrusting go-go boys or hilariously lame drag shows. Watch out for 801 club drag pensioner Margot!

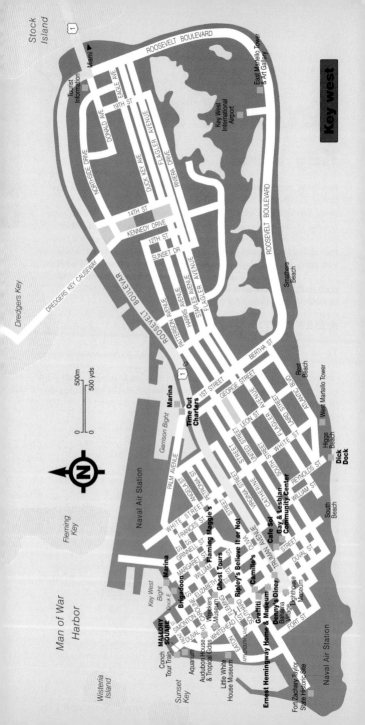

Key West

Stock Island

ROOSEVELT BOULEVARD
Miami ▶
Tourist Information

East Martello Tower & Art Gallery

19TH ST
EAGLE AVE
DONALD AVE
NORTHSIDE DRIVE
DUCK KEY AVE
FLAGLER AVENUE
RIVIERA DRIVE

Key West International Airport

14TH ST
KENNEDY DRIVE
12TH ST
SUNSET DR

ROOSEVELT BOULEVARD

DREDGERS KEY CAUSEWAY

Dredgers Key

ROOSEVELT BOULEVARD
PATTERSON AVENUE
HARRIS AVENUE
STAPLES AVENUE
FLAGLER AVENUE

Smathers Beach

500m
500 yds

Garrison Bight

Time Out Charters
Marina

1

1ST STREET
GEORGE STREET
BERTHA ST

Rest Beach

West Martello Tower

PALM AVENUE

N

Naval Air Station

VIRGINIA STREET
UNITED STREET
LEON STREET
ATLANTIC BLVD
FLAGLER

Higgs Beach

Dick Dock

Man of War Harbor

Fleming Key

WHITE STREET
FRANCES STREET
ANGELAST
PETRONIA STREET
Flaming Maggie's

REYNOLDS ST
WILLIAM ST

South Beach

Key West Bight
Marina
Dock E

Brigadoon
GRINNELL ST
MARGARET STREET
WILLIAM STREET
Ghost Tours
Camille's
Ripley's Believe It or Not

Gay & Lesbian Community Center
Cafe Sol
TRUMAN AVENUE

Wisteria Island
Sunset Key

Conch Tour Train
Aquarium
MALLORY SQUARE

SIMONTON STREET
CAROLINE ST
ELIZABETH ST
EATON
FLEMING ST
SOUTHARD
CATHERINE STREET
OLIVIA STREET
SOUTH STREET
WHITE STREET

Grafitti
Denny's Diner
Banana
DUVAL ST

Audubon House & Tropical Gdns
Little White House Museum
Wreckers Museum

APPROACH
DUVAL
MEDIVAL ST
WHITEHEAD ST

Ernest Hemingway Home & Museum

Lighthouse Museum
Village
FORT ST

Fort Zachary Taylor State Historic Site

Naval Air Station

OUTLINES

CONCH BIKE EXPRESS

- 305-294-4318
- 9am–5pm daily
- $12 per day; $35 per week

On yer bike for one of the best ways to get about. The cruiser bicycles come with a basket, lock and lights, with free delivery and pick-up to your hotel.

GAY & LESBIAN COMMUNITY CENTER

- 1075 Duval Street, Unit C-14
- 305-292-3223

www.glcckeywest.org
- 10am–9pm Mon–Sat; 1–5pm Sun

Free information on the local gay scene.

MALLORY SQUARE

- Between Whitehead & Duval Streets

A waterfront mecca crammed with kitsch gift shops, restaurants, juice bars and attractions. Buy shark jaws, or pet live ones at the Aquarium (1 Whitehead Street; 10am–6pm daily. Feedings 11am, 1, 3 & 4.30pm) or relive the town's pirate past at Key West

Shipwreck Historium (1 Whitehead Street; 9.45am–4.45pm daily).

RIPLEY'S BELIEVE IT OR NOT ODDITORIUM

- 527 Duval Street
- 305-293-9686
- 9am–11pm daily
- $11.95

Should there be an overcast day or a tropical downpour, here's somewhere silly to pass a few hours, with 1,500 exhibits including a two-headed calf, hurricane tunnel and Ernest Hemingway's high-school yearbooks.

The weird and the wonderful

Any colour you like...

All Shopped Out

Here there's plenty to see, but not much worth buying. For gay mags, books, cards and gifts Flaming Maggie's bookstore has got to be on your agenda. Likewise, The Leather Master might be useful if you're planning a visit to the town's only leather bar The One Saloon. Stores like Graffiti provides sexy swimwear and carnival-style clubwear for unashamed exhibitionists, and In Touch some jokey queer gifts to take back home. The main thoroughfare around Duval Street is home to familiar name stores like Banana Republic – in case you forgot to pack anything. Otherwise wade through the squillion small businesses crammed with antiques, arts, crafts and novelties – all designed to part us tourists from our money.

Top of the Shops

Graffiti

🛈 701 Duval Street, Key West. *See map p. 112*
📷 305-294-8040
🕙 10am–11pm daily

Great menswear shop right among the main drag on Duval Street. Two floors of underwear, swimwear and clubwear. Downstairs, sensible T-shirts, 2(x)ist and Calvin Klein, while upstairs things get decidedly camp and trashy with silver-sequined jockstraps ($22–$25) and the like. But where you'd wear one in dressed-down, laid-back Key West is anyone's guess.

Flaming Maggie's

🛈 830 Fleming Street, Key West. *See map p. 112*
📷 305-294-3931
🕙 10am–7pm daily

Sleepy gay bookshop and coffee-store stocking a completely impressive range of cards, gay fiction and art books, magazines and porn. Expect everything from *Inches* to *(not only) blue*. Pick out some postcards to send back home while you're here, and find a book to enthral you beside the pool. Definitely one to seek out.

Leather Master

ℹ 418a Applerouth Lane, Key West **|☎** 305-292-5051
www.leathermaster.com **|⌚** 11am–11pm Mon–Sat; noon–6pm Sun

About the only shop of its kind we could find. Luckily it's a good one,
well-stocked with leather and rubber wear, harnesses, porn DVDs, toys and
accessories, condoms and lube. The staff are friendly and helpful, but half
this stuff is far too hot to wear in this climate.

World of leather

Pandemonium

ℹ 825 Duval Street, Key West. *Duval
Street: see map p. 112.* **|☎** 305-294-5506
|⌚ 10am–10pm daily

Urbane gifts, local arts and crafts and
unusual jewellery. We liked the
cufflinks made out of old typewriter
keys ($45 a pair). You can't miss the
shop – theres a car covered in
mosaic tiles parked outside.

Take home some souvenirs

CYBERPORT KEY WEST

ⓘ 700 Front Street, Old Town, Key West
☎ 305-293-1313
🕐 9am–9pm daily

Shop online, surf the internet, check your emails or enter the chat rooms in privacy. Or play video games (great during an unexpected downpour), watch movies on DVD or rent a digital camera to capture a few memories of your stay in the Keys.

IN TOUCH

ⓘ 715 Duval Street, Key West
☎ 305-292-7293
🕐 9.30am–11pm daily

Funny, raunchy and downright rude gay greetings cards. Don't send one to Aunty Ethel. Not to mention novelties, gifts and rather tacky clubwear. T-shirts ($18) are of the 'Ward 2A Drama Queen Rehab' slogan variety if that's your thing.

PELICAN POOP SHOPPE

ⓘ 314 Simonton Street, Key West
☎ 305-296-3887
www.pelicanpoop.com
🕐 10am–6pm daily

Resembling a strange carved tropical jungle, Pelican Poop Shoppe is the place to pick up quirky, carved and painted decorative rainforest-themed gifts for the folks back home. It's also the site of Hemingway's first home in Key West, and the place where he wrote *A Farewell to Arms*.

Shop Around

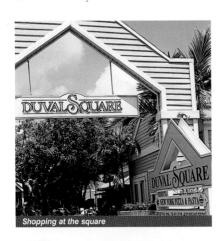

Shopping at the square

The chi-chi Cafe Marquesa

Eating Out
Cream of the Cuisine

Cafe Sole

ℹ 1029 Simonton Street, Key West.
See map p. 112 **📷** 305-294-0230
www.cafesole.com **⏱** 5.30–10pm daily
🍴 **🍴**

Off the beaten track, but near the gay resorts. This place offers a provincial French menu featuring duck, steak and risotto as well as seafood and pasta. Brace your tastebuds for grilled shrimp with tomato and hazelnut sauce, conch carpaccio, *escargot, moules marinière*, grilled Floridian lobster thermidor, roast duck and tenderised filet mignon.

Cafe Marquesa

ℹ Marquesa Hotel, 600 Fleming Street, Key West **📷** 305-292-1244
⏱ 6.30–10.30pm **🍴** **🍴**

Yellow and gold washed walls and large mahogany-framed mirrors, stylistically, are just this side of Jackie Stallone. The food is just as fussy, with specialities like seared yellow-fin tuna, peppercorn-dusted and served with saffron risotto; crusted rack of lamb with rosemary natural demi-glace, with a creamy polenta and eggplant caponata. That last one will set you back $31. Expensive chi-chi dining for all you show-offs, near the Fleming Street gay guest house strip.

Camille's

ℹ 703 1/2 Duval Street, Key West.
See map p. 112 **📷** 305-296-4811
info@camilleskeywest.com
⏱ 8am–3pm daily; 6–10pm Tues–Sat
🍴 **🍴**

Storefront gay bistro plastered in vintage movie star publicity photos. Very popular with the locals, gay or straight, so you'll have to be quick or patient to get a table. Once you're in, expect a varied menu of grilled Portobello mushrooms, chicken salad with raisins, stone crab claws or conch critters with Key lime roulade. Best are the breakfasts. Try an 'Orgy of Benedicts' – a croissant or muffin smothered in Norwegian salmon, veggies, stone crab claw meat, pink shrimp and Key West lobster.

The following price guides have been used for eating out and indicate the price for a main course:

🍴 = cheap = under $10

🍴 = moderate = $10–$20

🍴 = expensive = over $20

Denny's Diner

ℹ️ 925 Duval Street. *See map p. 112* | 📞 305-294-5065 | 🕐 Open 24 hours | 🍴 🍽️

Authentic 1950s-style diner with vinyl bar stools, seating booths and walls plastered with kitsch neon clocks and photos of classic Mustangs. Elvis could walk in at any minute. He'd certainly favour the big servings of fast food, cherry pie and hot fudge sundaes. Feel those veins thicken!

Half Shell Raw Bar

ℹ️ Margaret Street at the Seaport.
Margaret Street: map p. 112
📞 305-294-7496
🕐 11.45am– 10pm Mon–Sun;
11.45am–10.30pm Fri and Sat
🍴 🍽️ – 🍽️

Bag a window seat in this bayside shack and you might spot fish feeding beneath the pier. Healthy options include oysters, steamed clams, shrimp, lobster, stone crab claws and conch salad; pretty much everything else is deep-fried.

Petronia's

ℹ️ 207 Petronia Street, Bahama Village
📞 305-293-8860
🕐 5pm–10pm daily
🍴 🍽️

Cheap, authentic Polish cuisine on the corner of Emma and Petronia Streets in leafy Bahama Village. Hearty specialities include breaded chicken, stroganoff, roulade, meatballs, *sauerkraut* and deliciously naughty *gelata* cake packed with fruit, cream and an extra helping of calories.

Willie T's

ℹ️ 525 Duval Street.
Duval Street: map p. 112
📞 305-294-7674
🕐 7.30pm–4am daily
(11–4am Wed)
🍴 $15

'Hemingway never ate here. Not even once' states the menu. A tropical garden terrace, with fig trees teeming with fairylights, provides the setting and a vantage point

What's on the menu?

from which to watch the world pass by on Duval Street. Settle down to grilled country steak sandwiches and Caesar salads, or sweet potato fries in pepper gravy for a treat. Cheapish eats, great location.

Best of the Rest

ANTONIA'S

 615 Duval Street
305-294-6565
www.antoniaskeywest.com
6.30–11pm daily

Serving homemade Italian cuisine in Key West for over 20 years, this gay-friendly restaurant is a local landmark and one of the places to seek out.

CAFE EUROPA

1075 Duval Street
305-296-0266
www.CafeEuropa
KeyWest.com
8am–10pm daily

The intimate tropical garden setting for food with a casual European style. Enjoy European and American breakfasts, lunch or dinner in a bistro strewn with local arts and crafts.

HARD ROCK CAFE

 313 Duval Street
305-293-0230
www.keywest.com/hardrock
.html
11am–midnight daily

You know the drill. Cheapish classic American menu in a three-storey rock 'n' roll shrine overlooking Duval Street.

KELLY'S CARIBBEAN BAR GRILL

301 Whitehead Street
305-293-8484
www.kellyskeywest.com
noon–10pm daily

Owned by actress Kelly McGillis, with a Caribbean-flavoured, tapas-style menu. There's usually late-night entertainment, but, please don't get drunk and break into *Take My Breath Away*.

ROOFTOP CAFE

310 Front Street
305-294-2042
9am–10.30pm daily

Seafood, pasta and homemade desserts with outdoor seating overlooking historic old Key West. Handy for the nightly Sunset Celebration.

LA TRATTORIA

 524 Duval Street
305-296-1075
5.30pm–11pm daily

Award-winning Italian-French place frequented by locals: a good sign. There's an intimate smaller room, and a large and rowdy room, for a choice of ambience.

And another one flew by at the Fantasy Fest

Out on the Town

Sleepy Key West wakes up a little in the evenings – but not much. Nightlife here is bubbly rather than frenetic; you're not going to have the most hedonistic night of your life here. However there are a smattering of themed gay bars boasting drag, music videos, go-go boys and leather around Duval Street. Their close proximity makes it easy to circulate between them. Sunday sees a more energetic free T-Dance besides the ocean at the Atlantic Shores Resort just down the road.

My Top Clubs

801 Bourbon Bar

801 Duval, Street Key West. *Duval Street: map p. 112* No phone
11am–4am Mon–Sat; noon–4am Sun Free

Social gay gathering on the bar stools surrounding the large, circular main bar, with One Saloon leather bar through western-style doors out the back and drag cabaret upstairs. Actually, upstairs drag is somewhat funnier than the Divas variety down the street, especially if you've been on the tequila all day. Watch out for Margot, a truly ancient drag queen, who must be applauded for remembering all the words, while the other younger ladies don't always. Take change and dollar bills – there's a collection after each performance. Casual dress; 20s–50s crowd.

Bourbon Street Pub

724 Bourbon Street, Key West 305-296-1992 email: bourbstpub@aol.com www.bourbonstreetcomplex.com 11am–4am daily Free

Big, noisy gay video joint over 5,000 square feet, with five bars, seven video screens, 12 bartenders (I counted) and 50,000 watts of commercial dance music, causing ten tons of gay booty to shake in unison. Or something like that. Out back there's a quieter open-air poolside bar to escape from the musical melee. Casually dressed locals and tourist crowd, in their 20s–50s.

One Saloon

ⓘ 504 Petronia Street, Key West.
Petronia Street: map p. 112
☎ 305-294-4737
www.801bourbon.com
🕐 11am–4am daily; noon–4am Sun
💲 Free

Levis and leather joint linked to the main bar at 801 Bourbon Street. It's really just one long narrow industrial-style bar room, with toilets and a dark room leading off the near end. Here you'll find bears, cubs, leather men, and chubs. Dress butch in jeans and T-shirt, but don't worry too much, the dress code isn't rigidly enforced – it's far too hot! Butch Levis and leather crowd, in their 30s, 40's and 50s.

Sunday Tea-Dance

ⓘ Atlantic Shores Resort, 510 South Street, Key West. *South Street: map p. 112*
☎ 305-296-2491
🕐 10am–11pm Mon–Sat; 7–11pm Sun
💲 Free

Dance yourself dizzy under the star-studded heavens in one of the most beautiful club settings. It's literally a pier and poolside bar overlooking the ocean. Magical and quite romantic with the ocean breeze tousling the tropical palm trees and ruffling your quiff, moustache (or perhaps hirsute back if you're one of those bear types). Dress casual, but take a shirt in case it's breezy. Casual and label crowd, 20s–40s.

Life's a drag

DIVA'S

ⓘ 711 Duval Street,
Key West
📞 305-292-8500
email: keywestdance@
aol.com
www.divaskeywest.com
🕐 noon–4am daily
💲 $3

Half-hearted lip-
synching dragsters,
interrupted only by
the frenetic dirty
dancing of a testo-
sterone interlude
provided by the go-
go boys from next
door. Attracts a
drunken but friendly
mixed/gay crowd.
Shows 10pm and
11.30pm. Pay one
entrance fee and you
can go into Dudes
next door for free.
Casual dress, 20s–50s
crowd.

DUDES

ⓘ 711 Duval Street,
Key West
📞 305-292-8500
email: keywestdance@
aol.com
🕐 9pm–4am daily
💲 $3

Key West's newest
gay man's go-go bar.
Has young, scantily-
clad chickens shaking
their funky thangs
for older lechers
on a nightly basis.
Take muchos dollar
bills to tip them. All
rather tacky, I
thought, but
you might enjoy
it. Admission also
grants free entry
through a
connecting door to
Diva's. Casual dress,
attracts the 20s–50s
crowd.

All Clubbed Out

Festivals & Annual Parties

FANTASY FEST

LATE OCTOBER

ⓘ PO Box 230, Key West, FL 33041
📞 305-296-1817
Fax: 305-294-3335
www.fantasyfest.net

The last week of
October sees ten
days and nights of
a New Orleans-
style Mardi Gras.

Water music

Bar work

Working Out

Yeah, like you're here to work up a sweat! Key West is the place to unwind, so do as the natives do and take it easy. OK, well if you absolutely have to... chances are that your resort will have some gym facilities. If not, you'll be able to get a day pass to some nearby gay resort that does, or you can visit Club Body Tech down on Duval Street. You don't really need to, for the best workout in town just forego cabs and explore Key West's beaches and streets on foot.

OUTLINES

THE CLINIC

ⓘ 1503 Government Road, Key West

☎ 305-295-7550

🕐 8am–6pm Mon–Fri, 9am–1pm Sat & Sun

💲 1st visit $90–$125; subsequent visits $75–$90

Not quite chilled-out enough? Then walk in for relaxing Swedish massage or neuro-muscular therapy. Very gay-friendly. No appointment necessary.

CLUB BODY TECH

ⓘ 1075 Duval Street, Key West

☎ 305-292-9683

🕐 6am–10pm Mon–Fri; 8am–8pm Sat; 9am–5pm Sun

💲 $12.90 for a day pass; $85 for a monthly pass

Work out at Key West's gayest gym.

Steam room, cardio machines, free weights, aerobics, cycles, certified personal trainers, and massage. Day passes available. 25% off with your room key or business card.

THE SOLAR SPA

ⓘ 2824 N Roosevelt Boulevard, Key West

☎ 305-295-7177

email: kwsolarspa@aol.com

🕐 9am–7pm Mon–Sat; 10pm–4am Sun

Treat yourself to de-stressing and detoxifying treatments for relaxing and renewing your mind, body and spirit. A whole range of treatments with prices to suit all pockets, including massage, manicures, pedicures and dermatology.

Make good use of that pool

At Equator – one of Key West's men-only resorts

Checking In

The gay resorts are one of the best things about Key West.
Enjoy your gay seclusion away from the bustle of Duval Street.

The Best Beds

Alexander House

ℹ️ 1118 Fleming Street. *Fleming Street: map p. 112*
📞 305-294-9919 www.alexg house.com
🛏️ ❷ – ❸

One of the country's top ten guest houses according to *Out* magazine, this is an elegant gay and lesbian B&B. Swimming pool and outdoor hot tub. Nudity okay on the private second- and third- level sundecks.

Big Ruby's

ℹ️ 409 Applerouth Lane
📞 305-296-2323 email: keywest@bigrubys.com www.big rubys.com
🛏️ ❷ – ❸

Stylish and well-furnished guest house in beautiful tropical grounds. It is a big hit with single guys. Lagoon-like pool, cable, videos, and in-house video library.

Coconut Grove

ℹ️ 817 Fleming Street. Fleming Street: map p. 112 📞 305-296-5107
www.coconutgrovekeywest.com 🛏️ ❶ – ❷

Great-value accommodation. The well-kept rooms are in a rambling, men-only period property with rooftop sundecks. There's a large heated pool, outdoor Jacuzzi, and rooftop sundeck. Conveniently situated on Fleming Street, the bookstore Flaming Maggie's and the Equator resort are nearby.

Equator

ℹ️ 818 Fleming Street. *Fleming Street: map p. 112* 📞 305-294-775
www.equatorresort.com 🛏️ ❷

The following price guides have been used for accommodation, per room per night :
❶ = cheap = under $75
❷ = moderate = $75 – $200
❸ = expensive = $200 and over

Great men-only resort. Clothing is optional and the rooms are modern and well furnished. Attentive live-in owners make you feel welcome, and communal breakfast and cocktail hour helps break the ice. There's a lush tropical courtyard, beautiful black-tiled pool and secluded eight-man whirlpool spa. All rooms have cable, phone and fridge. No smoking.

By the pool at Coconut Grove

Fleur de Key Guest House

ⓘ 412 Frances Street
📷 305-296-4719
www.fleurdekey.com
 ③

Luxurious gay and lesbian guest house behind a screen of tropical palms and lush vegetation. Clothing optional. Videos, sundeck, a large pool, and a huge, kidney-shaped Jacuzzi. Cafe Sole and Flaming Maggie's are nearby, and Duval Street's nightlife is a walkable five blocks away.

Fleur de Key

Island House

ⓘ 1129 Fleming Street. *Fleming Street: map p. 112* 📷 305-294-6284 email: www.islandhousekeywest.com
🛏 ② – ③

A gay-owned and managed men-only resort attracting a fine assortment of young bucks, daddies, bears and cubs. Clean simple rooms but great facilities: indoor gym, Jacuzzi, sauna, steam room, outdoor pool and sundeck, and naughty video room. Residents of other establishments come here on $10 day passes, which must say something. Clothing optional.

Lighthouse Court

ⓘ 902 Whitehead Street, Key West. *Whitehead Street: map p. 112*
📷 Tel: (305) 294 9588
www.lighthousecourt.com
Fax: (305) 294 6861
Daily Rates: Peak Season
(21 Dec-30 April)
🛏 ② – ③
Off Season (1 May-20 Dec)
🛏 ① – ② Men only

The sign on reception said 'Back in a flash', and the hot conciërge actually did flash on his return, perfectly setting the flirtatious tone of this character-ful clothing-optional resort. Situated beside an old light-house and opposite historic Hemingway House, the largest all-male resort boasts a swimming pool, gym, huge two-level sundeck, small café and large jacuzzi spa. Rooms are simple, but this place is big on atmosphere.

Sleeping Around

CURRY HOUSE

 806 Fleming Street,
Key West

 305-294-6777

email: currygh@aol.com

www.gaytraveling.com/curr
yhouse

Fax: 305-294-5322

A beautiful period
town-house setting
for this small, well-
renovated, men-only,
gay-run guest house,
with a youngish
atmosphere that
makes it a hit with
party boys. Rooms
are well-furnished
and quite luxurious
for the money,
although the vaulted
roof in Room 9 – a
converted attic – is
a little on the
cramped side. It's
clothing optional
beside the large
pool and wooden
sundeck, there's
an outdoor hot
tub, and all rooms
have fridges and
air-conditioning.

DUVAL
HOUSE

 815 Duval Street,
Key West

Relax at your resort

305-294-1666

www.duvalhousekey
west.com

Fax: 305-292-1701

Mixed but very
gay-friendly guest
house which has
the advantage of
being smack in the
middle of Duval
Street, well within
crawling distance
back from all of
the bars, clubs,
shops and eateries.
Yet the place itself
is sedate and
secluded from
all the hullabaloo.
Ideally situated for
the especially laid
back.

PEARL'S
RAINBOW

 525 United Street,
Key West

305-292-1450

www.pearlsrainbow.com

Fax: 305-292-8511

Women-only,
Caribbean-American
lady's guest house
with two clothing-
optional swimming
pools and two hot
tubs, breakfast, and
poolside bar –
Pearl's Patio.
Centrally situated
very near all the
shops and action
of Duval Street
and just two blocks
from the ocean.

Easy Rider

Check This Out

Facts and tips for a stress free visit

Getting There

Whether your final destination is Miami Beach, Key West or Fort Lauderdale, as an international traveller you'll enter the country at Miami International Airport. Fort Lauderdale is a half-hour cab ride from Miami International Airport, and despite having its own airport – Fort Lauderdale/Hollywood International Airport – it actually handles only a limited amount of international flights. That's no problem though. And don't worry about a connecting flight to Fort Lauderdale – it's so close you should just take a 30-minute cab ride from right outside Miami International. Key West International Airport isn't international at all: it's only serviced by internal US airlines. You can get a connecting flight from Miami airport straight into Key West. It takes less than an hour and flights are frequent. Alternatively, you might find it fun to hire a car and drive down along the Overseas Highway. It takes about three hours, and some of the scenery en route is spectacular. If you arrive by plane you'll need to take a cab from Key West International Airport (on the southeastern tip of the island), across to Key West Old Town.

AIRPORTS

Miami International Airport: 876-7000

Fort Lauderdale/Hollywood International Airport: 359-6100

Key West International Airport: 296-5439

CONNECTING FLIGHTS TO KEY WEST

Among the best and most frequent airlines flying into Key West International Airport are United Airlines/American Eagle (tel: 1-800- 433-7300) and US Airways (tel: 1-800-428- 4322).

You can even book your connecting flight online at www.airnav.com/reserve/air

AIRPORT TO CITY TAXI FARES

Miami International Airport to Miami Beach approx $27.

Miami International Airport to Fort Lauderdale approx $70.

Key West International Airport to Key West Old Town approx $9-$12.

TAXI FIRMS

Miami – Central Cabs: 532-5555

Fort Lauderdale – Checker Taxis: 923-9999

Key West – Yellow Cabs: 444-4444

Tyres and taxis

CAR RENTALS

 Avis: 1-800-331-1212
 Budget: 1-800-527-0700
 Hertz: 1-800-654-313

BUDGET TRAVEL

 Campus Travel: 020-7730-2101
 STA Travel: 020-7361-6262
 Trailfinders: 020-7937-5400

TOUR OPERATORS

UK

 Airtours: 01706-260-0000
 British Airways: 01293-723-110
 Virgin Holidays: 01293-617-181

AIRLINES

UK

 Air Canada: 0990-247-226
 American Airlines: 020-8572-5555

 British Airways: 0345-222-111
 Continental: 0800-776-464
 Delta: 0800-414-767
 United: 0845-8444-777
 Virgin Airlines: 0800-747-747

USA

 Air Canada: 1-800-776-3000
 American Airlines: 1-800-433-7300
 Canadian Airlines: 1-800-426-700
 Continental Airlines: 1-800-525-0280
 KLM: 1-800-225-2525
 TWA: 1-800-221-2000
 United Airlines: 1-800-241-6522
 US Airways: 1-800-428-4322

AUSTRALIA

 Air New Zealand tel: 13 2476
 Cathay Pacific tel: 13 1747
 Delta: 1-800-251-878
 Quantas: 13-1211
 Singapore, Airlines tel: 13-1011
 United Airlines: 13-1777

REPUBLIC OF IRELAND

Aer Lingus (Belfast): 0645-737-747

Delta Airlines (Dublin): 1800-768-080

Thomas Cook: 01232-554-455

GAY TRAVEL

GOOD TIME GAY PRODUCTIONS, INC. (USA)

1-888-429-3527

www.goodtimegaytravel.com

PRIDE TRAVEL (AUSTRALIA)

1-800-061-427

PINK POUND TRAVEL BY DOVEHOUSE TRAVEL (UK)

0121-705-8141

www.pinkpoundtravel.com

TRAVEL CONTACTS FOR THE DISABLED

USA: SOCIETY FOR THE ADVANCEMENT OF THE HANDICAPPED

347 5th Avenue, New York, USA

212-447-7284

Non-profit advice and referral service.

UK: RADAR

12 City Forum, 250 City Road EC1 8AS 0207-250-3222

Free travel advice for the disabled.

AUSTRALIA: AUSTRALIAN COUNCIL FOR THE REHABILITATION OF THE DISABLED

PO Box 60 Curtain Road, Act 2605, Australia 06-682-4333

PASSPORTS AND VISAS

Visitors from the countries below spending less than 90 days in the US just need to complete the visa waiver and customs declaration given to you during your flight. Visitors from Australia and other countries may need to fill in a non–immigrant visitor's visa in advance. Your travel agent will advise you, and give you the application forms. Otherwise it is best to contact your nearest US Embassy or Consulate in plenty of time.

Visitors need to complete a visa waiver if they are from: UK, Austria, Andorra, Belgium, Brunei, Denmark, Finland, France, Germany, Iceland, Ireland, Italy, Japan, Luxembourg, Monaco, Liechtenstein, the Netherlands, New Zealand, Norway, San Marino, Spain, Sweden, Switzerland.

Visitors need to apply for a non–immigrant visitor's visa in advance if they are coming to the US from Australia and other countries not listed above.

CUSTOMS

US visitors are required to have a current passport and proof of return travel. You'll be required to fill in a customs declaration. These will be given to you on the plane, and basically ask you to state that you are not bringing in outlawed goods – there's a complete list on the form. You'll also have to fill in a visa waiver which asks you if you're in town for business or on holiday, where you'll be staying first of all, and your departure date. So make sure you have your hotel address and all the information you'll need with you on the aeroplane.

Airport tax is included in the price of your ticket, so there's no extra to pay. When you go through

CHECK THIS OUT

customs, give them your passport, the visa waiver and the customs declaration forms. They'll check your passport and might ask you a few questions about your trip.

HIV AND CUSTOMS

Horror stories persist of people with HIV being refused entry into the US. How true these stories are is unclear, but the customs declaration you have to fill in on arrival does ask you to state whether or not you suffer from any communicable disease (tick 'yes' or 'no'). Ask your doctor for advice here. One big giveaway could be the anti-viral medication you may have to take every day, which could be found in your luggage if you are searched by customs.

Some people prefer to contact a local HIV/AIDS organisation before they depart, and arrange to post the medication on ahead of them. You then just collect it on arrival at your destination. Your gay guest house might be prepared to do this also. If you'd prefer to go through an HIV/AIDS organisation, a good starting point is either the South Florida AIDS Network: tel: 305-585-7744 or Florida AIDS Action, tel: 305-891-3666. Explain the situation and they'll happily refer you to a local organisation.

In the City

TOURIST OFFICES AND INFORMATION

MIAMI CONVENTION AND VISITORS' CENTER
ℹ Suite 2700, 701 Brickell Avenue

What would you like to know?

☎ 305-539-3084
www.tropicoolmiami.com

GREATER FORT LAUDERDALE CONVENTION AND VISITORS' BUREAU
ℹ 1850 Eller Drive, Suite 303
☎ 954-765-4466 www.sunny.org

LESBIAN & GAY COMMUNITY CENTER KEY WEST
ℹ PO Box 71, Key West, 33041-0071
☎ 305-292-3223

GAY & LESBIAN CENTER OF SOUTH FLORIDA
ℹ 1717 North Andrews Avenue, Fort Lauderdale
☎ 954-563-9500
email: staff@glccftl.org

KEY WEST GAY BUSINESS GUILD
ℹ PO Box 1208, Key West, FL 33040
☎ 305-294-4603
email keywestgay@aol.com

ACCOMMODATION

South Florida is very gay-friendly, so sharing a room with a same-sex partner shouldn't cause eyebrows to raise. However, a good way to get the most up-to-date information on where to go and what to see is to stay at a gay resort or guest house. Staff and regular visitors are usually more than happy to give you the scoop.

PUBLIC TRANSPORT

Both South Beach and Key West are easily explored on foot. Given its sprawl, most people in South Florida are car owners, so the public transport system is minimal. If you want to really rove around, my advice is to hire a car. Your resort or landlord will advise you on the best firms. For shorter trips just take a cab. Taxis aren't meant to pick you up off the street, but if you try hailing some will invariably stop. When booking a taxi, the cab controller may ask, not for your address, but just for the phone number that you're calling from. Many firms can automatically call up your address that way, but it's bemusing the first time. After dining out or visiting a bar or nightclub, don't wander off into the street looking to hail a cab. Just ask the bartender or waiter to order a cab for you, then wait by the door. This is common practice, and they'll always be happy to oblige. Don't forget to tip the driver 15% on top of your fare.

CAR HIRE

If you do decide you want to hire a car and save on those taxi fares, then it is worth remembering that you can save time (and money) by arranging your car hire before you arrive in the US. Always ensure

Florida accommodation

CHECK THIS OUT

that any deal includes local taxes and insurance. While on that subject, it is imperative that you have adequate insurance for your rental car – don't just go for the legal minimum. As well as Collision Damage Waiver (CDW) or Loss Damage Waiver as it is sometimes called, take out Supplementary Liability Insurance (SLI) to ensure you have sufficient third-party liability.

A few more driving no-nos:

Don't attempt to drive on unfamiliar roads after a long flight – better to collect the car the next day.

Don't leave your car if hit by another car. Indicate for the other driver to follow you to a well-lit and busy area.

Don't even think of drinking and driving.

USEFUL NUMBERS

Avis 1-800-230-4898 www.avis.com
Budget 1-800-527-0700
www.budget.com
Enterprise 1-800-325-8007
Hertz 1-800-654-3131

CLIMATE

South Florida has a subtropical climate with annual average daily temperatures about 23°C (75°F). It's often referred to as the 'American Riviera' because many Americans travel down here to enjoy the surf and year-round sunshine. During the off-peak summer season temperatures often exceed the 33°C mark, and there can be heavy humidity. US visitors generally avoid the worst heat and humidity, so South Florida's peak season is really from November to March when temperatures are in the more bearable mid 20s and humidity is low. It's not known as the Sunshine State for nothing.

AVERAGE TEMPERATURES

MIAMI & FORT LAUDERDALE

January	68°F	20°C
February	69°F	21°C
March	72°F	22°C
April	75°F	24°C
May	78°F	26°C
June	81°F	27°C
July	82°F	28°C
August	84°F	29°C
September	80°F	27°C
October	78°F	26°C
November	73°F	23°C
December	70°F	21°C

KEY WEST

January	68°F	20°C
February	71°F	21°C
March	74°F	23°C
April	77°F	26°C
May	79°F	26°C
June	83°F	28°C
July	84°F	29°C
August	85°F	29°C
September	84°F	29°C
October	80°F	27°C
Novmber	75°F	24°C
December	72°F	22°C

EMBASSIES AND CONSULATES

AUSTRALIAN CONSULATE

2525 SW 3rd Avenue, Suite 410
Miami Florida 33129
305-858-7633 Fax: 305-857-0044

Highway patrol

POLICE & CRIME

Call free 911 from any telephone in case of emergencies. Be ready to give them your location, stay calm, pick up the receiver and dial. The operator will connect you to police, fire or ambulance.

DRUGS

Drugs are rife in South Florida, but anti-drug laws are some of the toughest in the US. On the dance-club circuit Crystal Meth (an amphetamine), X (ecstasy) and Cannabis are the recreational drugs of choice. All are illegal. So if you are caught with these or any illegal substances in your possession you will be dealt with severely – risking jail, deportation and a ban from entering the US.

BRITISH CONSULATE

305-374-1522 Fax: 305-374-8196
www.britain-info.org/consular/miami

CANADIAN CONSULATE

15 Floor, First Union Financial Center, 200 South Biscayne Boulevard, Miami, FL 33133
305-579-1600 Fax: 305-374-6774

Safety first

SAFETY AND SECURITY

It has to be stressed that while all three destinations are very gay-friendly, you should always keep your eyes open and err on the side of caution if you're not sure. Certain poorer parts of mainland Miami and Fort Lauderdale can be dodgy, so be sure to check your route if you're driving at night, take a cab or take someone who knows the area. If you're heading for a tourist attraction, keep your car doors locked and your eyes on the clearly marked routes. Steer clear of neighbourhoods which look rundown or have boarded-up windows, and keep going. Do not stop to ask directions. Keep your money concealed, don't carry large amounts of cash, and always act like you know where you're going. It's common sense really. South Florida is no more dangerous than most other US states and cities, London or Sydney, so if you stay aware of your surroundings and behave sensibly you should have no problems.

HEALTH

Although not officially compulsory, it's absolutely crucial to take out travel insurance. This should at least cover potential medical bills, and loss of baggage and belongings. There is no national health provision in the US, medical treatment is private, and should you be taken ill, doctors will treat first and bill later. Private medical bills can be astronomical, so don't risk travelling without health insurance cover. Some insurers won't cover people with HIV. So if you're HIV-positive you may want to take out cover with special insurers. Call your local gay switchboard for details of travel insurers covering people living with HIV and AIDS. In Europe, gay internet site Queercompany. com recently launched one such gay-friendly travel insurance policy. It's one that doesn't discriminate on the grounds of sexuality or HIV status. Call the London office for details on 020-7729-5424 or access their website.

GAY GROUPS AND RESOURCES

GAY, LESBIAN AND BISEXUAL HOTLINE
305-759-3661

MIAMI AIDS HOTLINE
800-352-2437

SOUTH BEACH AIDS PROJECT
305-532-1033

FORT LAUDERDALE (BROWARD COUNTY) COMMUNITY HEALTHCARE OF BROWARD COUNTY
954-568-2929

Free and confidential HIV testing and counselling.

GAY AND LESBIAN SWITCHBOARD
954-563-9500

HEALTH LINK
954-565-8284

PWA COALITION OF BROWARD COUNTY
954-565-9119
Support and advice for people living with AIDS.

KEY WEST AIDS HELPLINE
800-640-3867 or 305-296-6196

GAY AND LESBIAN HELPLINE
305-296-4357
Free advice and referral service.

MEDIA

COLUMBIA FUN MAPS
www.funmaps.com

Free gay maps featuring the local accommodation, food and nightlife. Very handy to have in your pocket. Reading one in a bar might attract some curious locals, keen to help out, so it's also a good way to make new friends.

EXPRESS
1595 NE 26th Street, Wilton Manors
954-568-1880
www.expressgaynews.com

Free gay and lesbian newspaper covering all of South Florida. News, features, columnists and entertainment listings.

HOTSPOTS MAGAZINE
954-928-1862
www.hotspotsmagazine.com
Free listings magazine with a round-up of the gay bars, entertainment and clubbing from Miami and South Beach, Key West, Fort Lauderdale and areas.

MIAMIGO
1234 Washington Avenue, Suite 200202
305-532-5051 www.miamigo.com

Glossy, free, quality monthly featuring interviews and entertainment news from around Florida's gay scene.

OUTLOOK MAGAZINE
2410 Wilton Drive, Wilton Manors, Fort Lauderdale
954-567-1306
www.outlookflorida.com

Weekly, free gay listings magazine covering Fort Lauderdale, Tampa, Palm Beach and Miami.

COMMUNICATIONS

Emergencies 911
Local directory information 411
Operator 0

Keep in touch

CHECK THIS OUT

INTERNATIONAL TELEPHONE CODES

You can call from public phones at 25c a minute for local calls using 25c, 10c and 5c coins, but it's best to buy a phonecard from your local convenience store. Key in the code number on the card. The cards carry full instructions. Some public phones accept credit cards. Just swipe them through the slot and dial. For long distance calls dial 1 before the area code. For international calls dial 011 followed by the country code.

INTERNATIONAL DIALLING CODES

UK: 44; Australia: 61; New Zealand: 64; Germany: 49; Ireland: 353
Details of other country codes from the International Operator on 1-800-874-4000.

USEFUL WEBSITES

www.curvemagazine.com – women's entertainment magazine
www.gay.com – news, entertainment and chat for lesbians and gay men
www.gfn.com – Gay Financial Network: a gay business services directory
www.girlfriendsmag.com – lesbian culture and entertainment
www.lesbianation.com – news, entertainment, health and travel info for women
www.m4m4sex.com – chat room for men
www.members.aol.com/gmfla – Girth & Mirth's South Florida events for chubs and bears
www.outandabout.com – gay travel magazine Out & About rates Florida's gay accommodation, which helps you compare facilities and general cleanliness
www.out.com – men's entertainment site
www.partyfinder.com – directory of annual circuit parties in the USA
www.womeninthelife.com – interviews, news and stuff for women

CURRENCY, CREDIT CARDS AND BANKS

All bills look the same. The $1, $5, $10, $20, $50 and $100 bills are all the same size and green colour, which can make them hard to distinguish. Check carefully as you part with your money, especially when you're boozing and leaving the bartender frequent $1 tips. Most bank cards will work in the American ATM machines (check with your bank before you go), which makes it easy to draw out cash 24 hours a day.

The major credit cards are accepted at most shops and establishments. In fact, without one you may find it difficult to make a hotel reservation. As the major cards are so widely accepted, throughout this book we have only pointed out exceptions to this rule such as those bars and shops who will take cash only.

OPENING HOURS

Banks: Mon–Thu 10am–3pm, Fri 9am–6pm and Sat 9am–1pm.
Shops 11am/noon–10/11pm.
Tourist offices 9am–5pm.
Restaurants 11am-6pm for breakfast and lunch, 6–11pm/midnight for dinner.

PUBLIC HOLIDAYS

1 Jan	New Year's Day
3rd Mon in Jan	Civil rights activist Martin Luther King Day
12 Feb	Former president Abraham Lincoln's Birthday
3rd Mon in May	President's Day
Sun, Mar or Apr	Easter Day

Last Mon in May	Memorial Day
4 July	Independence Day
1st Mon in Sept	Labor Day
2nd Mon in Oct	Columbus Day
11 Nov	Veterans' Day
4th Thur in Nov	Thanksgiving Day
25 Dec	Christmas Day

SHOPPING

Marked prices don't include a 6% sales tax which is added to most goods before you pay.

TIME

South Florida is on Eastern Standard Time (EST), 5 hours behind Greenwich Mean Time (GMT).

ELECTRICITY

US sockets carry 110v and take two-pronged plugs. You can pick up international plug adaptors from the airport, but because of the difference in voltage, some electrical goods from the UK and other countries might not work. Check to see if they allow voltage adjustment before you leave.

TIPPING

It's customary to tip waiters, taxi drivers and bartenders. Tips make up the bulk of their wages and compensate for poor basic pay. In restaurants tip 15% of the bill, or 20% if you're dining somewhere upmarket. Tip bartenders $1 every time you visit the bar.

You have been warned ...

INDEX

INDEX

NOTEBOOK

NOTEBOOK

Name _____

Address _____

_____

_____

Tel _____

Fax _____

email _____

Name _____

Address _____

_____

_____

Tel _____

Fax _____

email _____

Name _____

Address _____

_____

_____

Tel _____

Fax _____

email _____

Name _____

Address _____

_____

_____

Tel _____

Fax _____

email _____

Name _____

Address _____

_____

_____

Tel _____

Fax _____

email _____

Name _____

Address _____

_____

_____

Tel _____

Fax _____

email _____

out AROUND

CONTACT LIST

Name

Address

Tel

Fax

email

Name

Address

Tel

Fax

email

Name

Address

Tel

Fax

email

Name

Address

Tel

Fax

email

Name

Address

Tel

Fax

email

Name

Address

Tel

Fax

email

CONTACT LIST

Name _____

Address _____

_____

_____

Tel _____

Fax _____

email _____

Name _____

Address _____

_____

_____

Tel _____

Fax _____

email _____

Name _____

Address _____

_____

_____

Tel _____

Fax _____

email _____

Name _____

Address _____

_____

_____

Tel _____

Fax _____

email _____

Name _____

Address _____

_____

_____

Tel _____

Fax _____

email _____

Name _____

Address _____

_____

_____

Tel _____

Fax _____

email _____

OUT AROUND CONTACT LIST

Name _____   Name _____

Address _____   Address _____

_____   _____

_____   _____

Tel _____   Tel _____

Fax _____   Fax _____

email _____   email _____

Name _____   Name _____

Address _____   Address _____

_____   _____

_____   _____

Tel _____   Tel _____

Fax _____   Fax _____

email _____   email _____

Name _____   Name _____

Address _____   Address _____

_____   _____

_____   _____

Tel _____   Tel _____

Fax _____   Fax _____

email _____   email _____

MY TOP RESTAURANTS

Fill in details of your favourite restaurants below . . .
Tell us about them by logging on to **www.outaround.com**

Restaurant

Contact Details

Comments

Restaurant

Contact Details

Comments

Restaurant

Contact Details

Comments

My Top Restaurants

MY TOP BARS

Fill in details of your favourite bars below . . .
Tell us about them by logging on to **www.outaround.com**

My Top Bars

Bar

Contact Details

Comments

Bar

Contact Details

Comments

Bar

Contact Details

Comments

Fill in details of your favourite clubs below . . .
Tell us about them by logging on to **www.outaround.com**

My Top Clubs

Club

Contact Details

Comments

Club

Contact Details

Comments

Club

Contact Details

Comments

AMSTERDAM

LONDON

MIAMI

NEW YORK

PARIS

SAN FRANCISCO

Out AROUND

**Look for the
Rainbow Spine!**

Thomas Cook Publishing

**Your Gay Guide
to the World!**

The **Pink Paper**

Please help us update future editions by taking part in our reader survey. Every returned form will be acknowledged and to show our appreciation we will send you a voucher entitling you to £1 off your next Out Around guide or any other Thomas Cook guidebook ordered direct from Thomas Cook Publishing. Just take a few minutes to complete this form and return it to us.

Alternatively you can visit www.outaround.com and email us the answers to the questions using the numbers given below.

We'd also be glad to hear of your comments, updates or recommendations on places we cover or you think that we ought to cover.

1   Which Out Around guide did you purchase?

2   Have you purchased other Out Around guides in the series?

☐ Yes ☐ No   If Yes, please specify

3   Which of the following tempted you into buying your Out Around guide. (Please tick as appropriate)

☐ The price
☐ The rainbow spine
☐ The cover
☐ The fact it was a dedicated gay travel guide
☐ Other

4   Please rate the following features of your 'Out Around guide' for their value to you (circle VU for 'very useful', U for 'useful', NU for 'little or no use')

'A Day Out' features	VU	U	NU
Top Sights	VU	U	NU
Top restaurants and cafés and listings	VU	U	NU
Top shops and listings	VU	U	NU
Top hotels and listings	VU	U	NU
Top clubs and bars and listings	VU	U	NU
Theatre and music venues	VU	U	NU
Gyms and sauna choices	VU	U	NU
Practical information	VU	U	NU

FEEDBACK FORM

5   How did you book your holiday?

- [ ] Package deal
- [ ] Package deal through a gay-specific tour operator
- [ ] Flight only
- [ ] Accommodation only
- [ ] Flight and accommodation booked separately

6   How many people are travelling in your party?

7   Which other cities do you intend to/have travelled to in the next/past 12 months?

	Yes	No
Amsterdam	[ ]	[ ]
London	[ ]	[ ]
Miami	[ ]	[ ]
New York	[ ]	[ ]
Paris	[ ]	[ ]
San Francisco	[ ]	[ ]

Other (please specify)

8   Please tell us about any features that in your opinion could be changed, improved, or added in future editions of the book, or any other comments you would like to make concerning the book:

_____

_____

_____

_____

_____

From time to time we send our readers details of new titles or special offers. Please tick here if you wish your name to be held on our mailing list (Note: our mailing list is never sold to other companies). [ ]

Please detach or photocopy this page and send it to: The Editor, Out Around, Thomas Cook Publishing, PO Box 227, The Thomas Cook Business Park, Peterborough PE3 8XX, United Kingdom.

9   Your age category
[ ] under 21 [ ] 21-30 [ ] 31-40 [ ] 41-50 [ ] 51+

First name (or initials)

Last name

Your full address (Please include postal or zip code)

_____

_____

Your daytime telephone number:

_____